Contents

CONTENT CHART

GRAMMAR	READING	WRITING
• too … to / enough … to • Conjunctions: Although, But, Because, So	The Job of a Firefighter	Write a letter to your future self
• Modal Verbs	Yummy's Tex-Mex	Make a recommendation for a restaurant
• Adverbs of Frequency • Phrases of Frequency	Themed Races: Run for Fun	Write about what you usually do in your free time
• Infinitives and Gerunds • Stop / Remember / Forget + to V. / V-ing	Health Threats Caused by Electronic Devices	Write an e-mail to ask for sick leave
• Correlative Conjunctions	The Beautiful Guitar	Write about your daily life
• Sense Verbs • Reflexive Pronouns	How Horror Hooks and Helps Us	Asking someone to the movies by e-mail
• Dative Case • Conjunctive Adverbs: However	Yesterday's Technology Makes a Comeback	Inventing something to make life easier
• Noun Clauses	App Stickers' Popularity	Update your status on social network sites
• Linking Verbs • –ing adjectives VS. –ed adjectives	Positive Thinking	List your methods of getting happy
• Relative Pronouns	Arranged Marriage	Asking someone out by e-mail
• Relative Pronouns: Restrictive VS. Nonrestrictive	The King and His Two Wives	Write a fable with a different ending
• Adjective Complement • Subordinating Conjunctions: As Soon As	What Riddles Can Teach Us	Write your own riddles

LEARNING OVERVIEW

The Live Escalate series comes in three volumes, from Book 1: Base Camp to Book 3: Summit. Each book is made up of 12 units and a review section after every six units. The following is the introduction for Book 2: Trekking. There are reading, listening, writing, and speaking activities in each unit. Readers will be challenged by the variety of fun and interesting content throughout the series.

WARM UP

A warm-up section of the theme topic

Students start each lesson with critical-thinking questions. These thought-provoking questions will spark students' interest in the topic while also providing excellent speaking practice.

Students will strengthen their listening and speaking ability with these engaging activities. First is a listening comprehension quiz, which consists of three short talks or monologues. Next is a short role-play. Here, students will put their communication skills to the test in various real-life scenarios.

CONVERSATION

A dialogue about the theme topic with a variety of questions

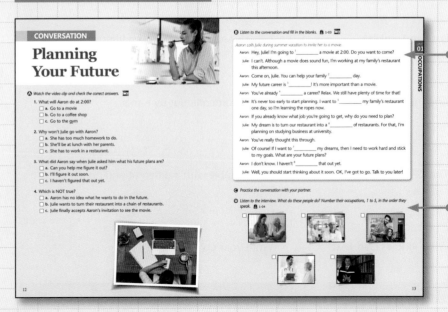

The dialogues use realistic, modern English to deliver practical and fun conversation practice.

Here, students will find various types of activities that will assess their understanding. Completing these tasks will help students feel confident in their English ability.

GRAMMAR
Explicit and lively grammar instruction through visuals

In this section, further information related to the grammar lesson is provided. The design, which resembles an instant-messaging service, is fun and relatable for students. They will feel like they have their own personal online tutor!

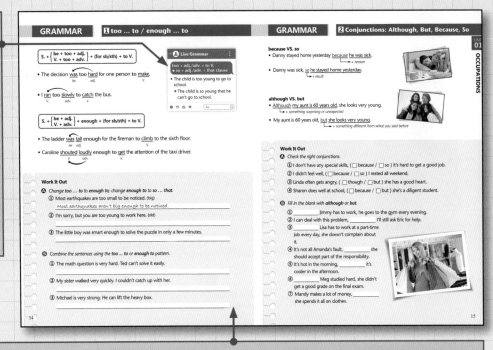

This quick and effective quiz provides students an instant assessment of what they've just learned. It also teaches them how and when to use the grammar points taught previously.

READING
An article about the theme topic with a variety of questions

The article features compelling topics and is filled with fascinating facts and information.

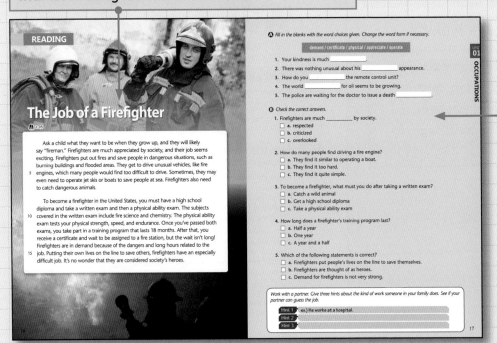

Students will check their comprehension with different types of review questions.

LEARNING OVERVIEW

WRITING

Read the sample article and write a letter to your future self. Share it with the class.

http://www.future.com

Dear future self,

My dream is to become a doctor. Maybe in 10 years we will be working for Doctors Without Borders and saving lives in an exciting foreign country!

Jenny Azure, 13 years old

Dear future self,

I got some teeth pulled last week, and it was terrible. I decided right then and there that I would become a dentist so I could make others feel the same horrible pain I did.

Trista Coughlin, 12 years old

Dear future self,

I think the best job is to be a backpacker. I could travel around the whole world, working in every country and getting a taste of what it's like before moving on. Now that's my kind of job!

Mike Hayden, 14 years old

Think about ...
- Why you want the job
- Details about the job
- Why the job is fun/interesting
- Where you'll work
- How much money you'll make

WRITING

Real-life writing tasks, such as letters and essays

Useful sentence patterns and instructions are given to prompt students and get them started. Students will improve their writing skills while having fun along the way!

CHALLENGE YOURSELF

A topic-related listening test

This section provides an excellent tool for students to track their improvement and be aware of the improvement in their English proficiency.

CHALLENGE YOURSELF

UNIT 01

OCCUPATIONS

Part I Pictures 🎧 1-06

Look at the picture and choose the best answer.

1.

☐ a   ☐ b   ☐ c

2.

☐ a   ☐ b   ☐ c

Part II Question & Response 🎧 1-07

Listen to the statement or question and choose the best response.

3. ☐ a   ☐ b   ☐ c   5. ☐ a   ☐ b   ☐ c
4. ☐ a   ☐ b   ☐ c   6. ☐ a   ☐ b   ☐ c

Part III Conversations 🎧 1-08

Listen to the conversation and answer the questions.

7. What does the man want to know about Karen?
☐ a. What she does as a job
☐ b. If she's married or single
☐ c. What she likes to do for fun

8. What does the man want to do?
☐ a. Work in a library
☐ b. Study more about art
☐ c. Help people learn about art

9. Where does the woman work?
☐ a. At a theater
☐ b. In a restaurant
☐ c. At a hospital

10. What does the woman say about the party?
☐ a. It will start after eight o'clock.
☐ b. She's bringing a friend.
☐ c. There will be a lot of food.

Linguaporta Training

Let's review the unit with Linguaporta.

19

WELCOME TO *LIVE ESCALATE*!

The Live Escalate series comes in three volumes, from Book 1: Base Camp to Book 3: Summit. Each book is made up of 12 units and a review section after every six units. There are reading, listening, writing, and speaking activities in each unit. Readers will be challenged by the variety of fun and interesting content throughout the series.

A Complete Series

Each of the three books in this stimulating and pragmatic series is designed with a natural flow in mind: listening ⇨ speaking ⇨ reading ⇨ writing, with the result being that your English improves dramatically while you're unaware of the effort you've spent. The aim is that with minimal friction, learners of all ages will assimilate this language with the same fluidity a child does in his or her native environment, thus removing the sense of foreignness and frustration that is part of foreign language learning.

Unit Themes Focusing on Self-Expression

The units covered in this series pertain to ordinary life, focusing on the types of situations and challenges learners encounter every day, including shopping, eating, socializing, odds and ends around the house, leisure, and more.

Book 3: Summit
I CAN express opinions on some matters in a controlled way.

Book 2: Trekking
I CAN express opinions in a controlled way.

Book 1: Base Camp
I CAN take part in a conversation on a familiar topic.

Occupations

WARM UP

TALK ABOUT THIS

Talk about these questions.

Do you think it's better to have an easy job or a challenging job?

ACTIVATE

(A) *Listen to the short talks and choose the correct pictures.* 🎧 1-02

Question 1.

Question 2.

Does anyone in your family have an interesting job? If yes, what?

Question 3.

B *Role-play with a partner. Extend the conversation as much as you can.*

Ⓐ What does your father / mother do?

Ⓑ He / She is a(n) _____.

....

Ⓐ What are you going to be in the future?

Ⓑ I'm going to be a(n) _____.

Planning Your Future

A *Watch the video clip and check the correct answers.* WEB動画

1. What will Aaron do at 2:00?
   - ☐ **a.** Go to a movie
   - ☐ **b.** Go to a coffee shop
   - ☐ **c.** Go to the gym

2. Why won't Julie go with Aaron?
   - ☐ **a.** She has too much homework to do.
   - ☐ **b.** She'll be at lunch with her parents.
   - ☐ **c.** She has to work in a restaurant.

3. What did Aaron say when Julie asked him what his future plans are?
   - ☐ **a.** Can you help me figure it out?
   - ☐ **b.** I'll figure it out soon.
   - ☐ **c.** I haven't figured that out yet.

4. Which is NOT true?
   - ☐ **a.** Aaron has no idea what he wants to do in the future.
   - ☐ **b.** Julie wants to turn their restaurant into a chain of restaurants.
   - ☐ **c.** Julie finally accepts Aaron's invitation to see the movie.

B *Listen to the conversation and fill in the blanks.* 🎧 1-03 💻 WEB動画

Aaron calls Julie during summer vacation to invite her to a movie.

Aaron: Hey, Julie! I'm going to ¹_____ a movie at 2:00. Do you want to come?

Julie: I can't. Although a movie does sound fun, I'm working at my family's restaurant this afternoon.

Aaron: Come on, Julie. You can help your family ²_____ day.

Julie: My future career is ³_____! It's more important than a movie.

Aaron: You've already ⁴_____ a career? Relax. We still have plenty of time for that!

Julie: It's never too early to start planning. I want to ⁵_____ my family's restaurant one day, so I'm learning the ropes now.

Aaron: If you already know what job you're going to get, why do you need to plan?

Julie: My dream is to turn our restaurant into a ⁶_____ of restaurants. For that, I'm planning on studying business at university.

Aaron: You've really thought this through.

Julie: Of course! If I want to ⁷_____ my dreams, then I need to work hard and stick to my goals. What are your future plans?

Aaron: I don't know. I haven't ⁸_____ that out yet.

Julie: Well, you should start thinking about it soon. OK, I've got to go. Talk to you later!

C *Practice the conversation with your partner.*

D *Listen to the interview. What do these people do? Number their occupations, 1 to 5, in the order they speak.* 🎧 1-04

☐    ☐    ☐

☐    ☐

13

$$S. + \begin{Bmatrix} be + too + adj. \\ V. + too + adv. \end{Bmatrix} + (for\ sb/sth) + to\ V.$$

- The decision <u>was</u> **too** <u>hard</u> for one person **to** <u>make</u>.
  be   *adj.*   *V.*

- I <u>ran</u> **too** <u>slowly</u> **to** <u>catch</u> the bus.
  V.   *adv.*   *V.*

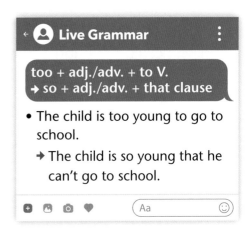

Live Grammar

too + adj./adv. + to V.
→ so + adj./adv. + that clause

- The child is too young to go to school.
  → The child is so young that he can't go to school.

Aa

$$S. + \begin{Bmatrix} be + adj. \\ V. + adv. \end{Bmatrix} + enough + (for\ sb/sth) + to\ V.$$

- The ladder <u>was</u> <u>tall</u> **enough** for the fireman **to** <u>climb</u> to the sixth floor.
  be   *adj.*   *V.*

- Caroline <u>shouted</u> <u>loudly</u> **enough to** <u>get</u> the attention of the taxi driver.
  V.   *adv.*   *V.*

Work It Out

A *Change* ***too … to*** *to* ***enough to***; *change* ***enough to*** *to* ***so … that***.

① Most earthquakes are too small to be noticed. (big)

   <u>Most earthquakes aren't big enough to be noticed.</u>

② I'm sorry, but you are too young to work here. (old)

   _____

③ The little boy was smart enough to solve the puzzle in only a few minutes.

   _____

B *Combine the sentences using the* ***too … to*** *or* ***enough to*** *pattern.*

① The math question is very hard. Ted can't solve it easily.

   _____

② My sister walked very quickly. I couldn't catch up with her.

   _____

③ Michael is very strong. He can lift the heavy box.

   _____

because VS. so
- Danny stayed home yesterday <u>because</u> <u>he was sick</u>.
  └──▶ + *reason*

- Danny was sick, <u>so</u> <u>he stayed home yesterday</u>.
  └──▶ + *result*

although VS. but
- <u>Although</u> <u>my aunt is 60 years old</u>, she looks very young.
  └──▶ + *something surprising or unexpected*

- My aunt is 60 years old, <u>but</u> <u>she looks very young</u>.
  └──▶ + *something different from what you said before*

Work It Out

Ⓐ *Check the right conjunctions.*

① I don't have any special skills, (☐ because / ☐ so) it's hard to get a good job.

② I didn't feel well, (☐ because / ☐ so) I rested all weekend.

③ Linda often gets angry, (☐ though / ☐ but) she has a good heart.

④ Sharon does well at school, (☐ because / ☐ but) she's a diligent student.

Ⓑ *Fill in the blank with **although** or **but**.*

① _____ Jimmy has to work, he goes to the gym every evening.

② I can deal with this problem, _____ I'll still ask Eric for help.

③ _____ Lisa has to work at a part-time job every day, she doesn't complain about it.

④ It's not all Amanda's fault, _____ she should accept part of the responsibility.

⑤ It's hot in the morning, _____ it's cooler in the afternoon.

⑥ _____ Meg studied hard, she didn't get a good grade on the final exam.

⑦ Mandy makes a lot of money, _____ she spends it all on clothes.

The Job of a Firefighter

🎧 1-05

Ask a child what they want to be when they grow up, and they will likely say "fireman." Firefighters are much appreciated by society, and their job seems exciting. Firefighters put out fires and save people in dangerous situations, such as burning buildings and flooded areas. They get to drive unusual vehicles, like fire
5 engines, which many people would find too difficult to drive. Sometimes, they may even need to operate jet skis or boats to save people at sea. Firefighters also need to catch dangerous animals.

   To become a firefighter in the United States, you must have a high school diploma and take a written exam and then a physical ability exam. The subjects
10 covered in the written exam include fire science and chemistry. The physical ability exam tests your physical strength, speed, and endurance. Once you've passed both exams, you take part in a training program that lasts 18 months. After that, you receive a certificate and wait to be assigned to a fire station, but the wait isn't long! Firefighters are in demand because of the dangers and long hours related to the
15 job. Putting their own lives on the line to save others, firefighters have an especially difficult job. It's no wonder that they are considered society's heroes.

Ⓐ *Fill in the blanks with the word choices given. Change the word form if necessary.*

> demand / certificate / physical / appreciate / operate

1. Your kindness is much _____.

2. There was nothing unusual about his _____ appearance.

3. How do you _____ the remote control unit?

4. The world _____ for oil seems to be growing.

5. The police are waiting for the doctor to issue a death _____.

Ⓑ *Check the correct answers.*

1. Firefighters are much _____ by society.
   - ☐ a. respected
   - ☐ b. criticized
   - ☐ c. overlooked

2. How do many people find driving a fire engine?
   - ☐ a. They find it similar to operating a boat.
   - ☐ b. They find it too hard.
   - ☐ c. They find it quite simple.

3. To become a firefighter, what must you do after taking a written exam?
   - ☐ a. Catch a wild animal
   - ☐ b. Get a high school diploma
   - ☐ c. Take a physical ability exam

4. How long does a firefighter's training program last?
   - ☐ a. Half a year
   - ☐ b. One year
   - ☐ c. A year and a half

5. Which of the following statements is correct?
   - ☐ a. Firefighters put people's lives on the line to save themselves.
   - ☐ b. Firefighters are thought of as heroes.
   - ☐ c. Demand for firefighters is not very strong.

Work with a partner. Give three hints about the kind of work someone in your family does. See if your partner can guess the job.

Hint 1   ex.) He works at a hospital.
Hint 2
Hint 3

17

WRITING

Read the sample article and write a letter to your future self. Share it with the class.

http://www.future.com

Dear future self,

My dream is to become a doctor. Maybe in 10 years we will be working for Doctors Without Borders and saving lives in an exciting foreign country!

Jenny Azure, 13 years old

Dear future self,

I got some teeth pulled last week, and it was terrible. I decided right then and there that I would become a dentist so I could make others feel the same horrible pain I did.

Trista Coughlin, 12 years old

Dear future self,

I think the best job is to be a backpacker. I could travel around the whole world, working in every country and getting a taste of what it's like before moving on. Now that's my kind of job!

Mike Hayden, 14 years old

Think about ...

- Why you want the job
- Details about the job
- Why the job is fun/interesting
- Where you'll work
- How much money you'll make

CHALLENGE YOURSELF

Part I **Pictures** 💿 1-06

Look at the picture and choose the best answer.

1.

☐ a   ☐ b   ☐ c

2.

☐ a   ☐ b   ☐ c

Part II **Question & Response** 💿 1-07

Listen to the statement or question and choose the best response.

3. ☐ a   ☐ b   ☐ c   5. ☐ a   ☐ b   ☐ c
4. ☐ a   ☐ b   ☐ c   6. ☐ a   ☐ b   ☐ c

Part III **Conversations** 💿 1-08

Listen to the conversation and answer the questions.

7. What does the man want to know
about Karen?
☐ a. What she does as a job
☐ b. If she's married or single
☐ c. What she likes to do for fun

8. What does the man want to do?
☐ a. Work in a library
☐ b. Study more about art
☐ c. Help people learn about art

9. Where does the woman work?
☐ a. At a theater
☐ b. In a restaurant
☐ c. At a hospital

10. What does the woman say about the
party?
☐ a. It will start after eight o'clock.
☐ b. She's bringing a friend.
☐ c. There will be a lot of food.

Linguaporta Training

Let's review the unit with Linguaporta.

At the Dinner Table

WARM UP

TALK ABOUT THIS

Talk about these questions.

What do you think is the most important etiquette rule?

ACTIVATE

A *Listen to the conversations and choose the correct pictures.* 🎵 1-09

Question 1.	Question 2.

Do you ever set the table at home?

B *Role-play with a partner. Extend the conversation as much as you can.*

Ⓐ May I take your order?

Ⓑ Yes, I'd like to have the _____, please.

....

Ⓐ What would you like to order?

Ⓑ I'd like the _____, please.

....

Ⓐ How would you like your steak?

Ⓑ I'd like my steak medium/well-done/rare.

Question 3.

First and Last Lunch Date

A *Watch the video clip and check the correct answers.* 🖥️ WEB動画

1. What is the most expensive entrée on the menu?
   - ☐ **a.** A garden salad
   - ☐ **b.** Filet mignon
   - ☐ **c.** The lobster dinner

2. Why is Sarah unhappy with Nick?
   - ☐ **a.** Because he started eating his entrée before she had her food.
   - ☐ **b.** Because he didn't let her choose which piece of garlic bread she wanted.
   - ☐ **c.** Because he didn't let her choose the most expensive main course.

3. Which piece of garlic bread would Sarah choose?
   - ☐ **a.** She would choose the smallest piece.
   - ☐ **b.** She would choose the biggest piece.
   - ☐ **c.** She would let Nick choose first.

4. Why doesn't Nick have many friends at school?
   - ☐ **a.** Because he only thinks about himself.
   - ☐ **b.** Because he never pays for lunch.
   - ☐ **c.** Because he eats too much garlic bread.

B *Listen to the conversation and fill in the blanks.* 🎧 1-10 💻 WEB動画

Nick and Sarah are classmates. Sarah wants to find out why Nick can't make any friends at school. She invites him out for lunch, and they go to a nearby restaurant.

Waiter: Excuse me, sir, madam. May I take your order?

Sarah: Yes. I'd like to have the garden salad, please. Nick, what would you like to order? Have whatever you like. I'm [1]_____.

Nick: Thank you, Sarah! I'd like the lobster dinner, please. And garlic bread as a [2]_____ order.

Sarah: (Shocked) Wow! Nick! You ... You chose the most expensive main course! (To the waiter) Well, I'll just [3]_____ his garlic bread. And just some water to drink, thanks.

Waiter: [4]_____ right up!

After a few minutes, the waiter returns with the water and garlic bread. One piece is much bigger than the other.

Waiter: Here you are. Your garlic bread to share. I'll just put this in the [5]_____.

Sarah: Oh, there are just two pieces of garlic bread.

Nick: Well, I'll take that piece. Mmm. Delicious!

Sarah: Nick! You took the biggest piece. That's very [6]_____. You should offer it to me first.

Nick: Oh, and, if I did, which piece would you take?

Sarah: I would be [7]_____ and take the smallest piece.

Nick: Well, that piece is still there. It's all [8]_____, Sarah.

Sarah: Nick! Well, I can now see why you can't make any friends at school!

C *Practice the conversation with your partner.*

D *Listen to the conversation and circle what the speaker orders.* 🎧 1-11

Appetizer	Main Course	Soup	Drink
Buffalo wings	spaghetti	French onion soup	coffee
potato skins	New York steak	tomato soup	black tea
cheese sticks	fish and chips	bean soup	orange juice

23

direct ← **can   could   may   might** → indirect, formal

can, could

- <u>Can</u> I sit here? = <u>May</u> I sit here?
  ↳ *to ask for and give permission*

- John said we <u>can/could</u> meet next week.
  ↳ *to make suggestion*

- A: <u>Could</u> I speak to Mr. Jones?
  ↳ *to express permission politely*

  B: I'm afraid he's out of the office right now.

may, might

- <u>May</u> I please have another piece of cake?
  ↳ *to ask for formal permission*

- The medicine <u>may</u> cure your cough.
  ↳ *to express possibility*

will, would, would like

- <u>Will</u> you shut the door, please?
  ↳ *to request someone to do something*

- <u>Would</u> you please do me a favor?

> **Would you mind +** { if + S. + V. / V-ing }

- <u>Would you mind if</u> I leave class early today?

- <u>Would you mind going</u> to the store to get some eggs?

Live Grammar

Modal Verb	Usage
can, could	ability
	permission
	possibility
may, might	permission
	possibility
should	advice

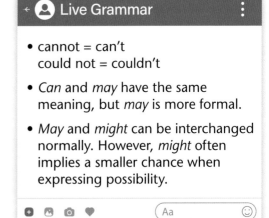

Live Grammar

- cannot = can't
  could not = couldn't

- *Can* and *may* have the same meaning, but *may* is more formal.

- *May* and *might* can be interchanged normally. However, *might* often implies a smaller chance when expressing possibility.

would like to V. = want to V.

• A: What would you like to order?
  ↳ to express desire politely

  B: I'd like the Caesar salad.

• A: Would you like some ice cream for dessert?

  B: No, thank you.

Work It Out

Ⓐ *Check the correct answers.*

① What club (☐ would you like / ☐ would you like to) join?

② I'm very sorry, Ms. White, but I (☐ have to / ☐ have) miss class next week.

③ You don't (☐ must / ☐ have to) decide now. Take your time.

④ (☐ Could I / ☐ Could you) borrow your pen?

⑤ (☐ I'd like / ☐ I'd like to) a table for four, please.

⑥ Dave is always telling lies. You (☐ should / ☐ shouldn't) believe him.

Ⓑ *Check the correct answers.*

① It's getting late, but he hasn't arrived yet.
   He (☐ may not / ☐ may) come over.

② Joe didn't go to school today. He might (☐ be / ☐ is) sick.

③ She may (☐ come / ☐ came), or she may
   (☐ come not / ☐ not come).

④ There is a lot of traffic, so we may (☐ are / ☐ be) late.

⑤ We (☐ might / ☐ might be) go to the movies tonight.

Ⓒ *Match the sentences.*

① May I take your order?   •   • Medium, please.

② Can I have another piece of pizza?   •   • Yes. I will.

③ Would you mind if I turn on the radio? •   • Sure. Help yourself.

④ How would you like your steak?   •   • Yes, I'd like a cheeseburger.

⑤ Will you buy me a drink?   •   • I'm sorry, but the baby is sleeping.

25

Yummy's Tex-Mex

1012 Dandelion Road, Houston, TX 77071
Phone: 555-642-0109

URL: www.yummytexmex.com
Price: $20–$40

Yummy's attracts passers-by with its large outdoor seating area decorated with flowers. The delicious smell of grilled steak coming from the kitchen will make you want to stay. The restaurant colors are warm and relaxing, from
5 yellow to orange. Red stone tiles and a brick wall full of wine add to the welcoming atmosphere.

I chose the Buffalo wings to start, the lobster dinner for a main course, and—my favorite as a child—the chocolate ice cream for dessert. The wings were beautifully presented.
10 Placed on a bed of lettuce and onions, they were served with yellow rice. The sauce was rich and delicious, just spicy enough to wake up but not burn my mouth.

The lobster, cooked in a spicy lemon-and-butter sauce, melted in my mouth but left a gentle, lasting flavor. The
15 chocolate ice cream, however, was lost beneath a mountain of cream.

Despite the disappointing ice cream, I'll definitely be back for more at Yummy's. Next time, I'll finish with the cheesecake.

A *Fill in the blanks with the word choices given. Change the word form if necessary.*

passer-by / atmosphere / disappointing / beneath / decorate

1. The cake was _____ to look like a castle.

2. A _____ saw smoke and called the fire department.

3. There's a very relaxed _____ in our office.

4. The film was really _____. It was a waste of time.

5. Ryan hid the letter _____ a pile of papers.

B *Check the correct answers.*

1. What makes passers-by not want to leave Yummy's?
   ☐ a. The indoor seating area
   ☐ b. The music coming from the restaurant
   ☐ c. The delicious smell of steak

2. Which is NOT something good about Yummy's?
   ☐ a. The colors
   ☐ b. The dessert
   ☐ c. The Buffalo wings

3. Which of the following is NOT true?
   ☐ a. The walls were painted yellow and orange.
   ☐ b. The writer won't be back at Yummy's.
   ☐ c. The chocolate ice cream was not very good.

4. How was the sauce on the Buffalo wings?
   ☐ a. Sour
   ☐ b. Spicy
   ☐ c. Salty

5. What was wrong with the chocolate ice cream?
   ☐ a. It came with too much whipped cream.
   ☐ b. The chocolate ice cream didn't have chocolate in it.
   ☐ c. The writer actually ordered the cheesecake.

Tell a partner about your favorite restaurant. Don't forget to talk about the dishes it serves.

N.Y. Gourmet
Burgers

No. 101, Sec. 6, Xin-Yi Rd.,
New York
Tel: 333-6000-0234

Name	Favorite Restaurant	Dishes
Kelly	BELLINI	pasta & pizza

Ⓐ *Complete the sentences with* **would you like, would you like to,** *or* **do you like.**

① A: _____ some coffee?

   B: Yes, I'd like to.

② A: _____ to play tennis?

   B: Yes, I do.

③ A: _____ play tennis on the weekend?

   B: Sure. What time?

④ A: What _____ order for the main dish?

   B: I want the steak.

Ⓑ *Look at the menu from the La Bamba Restaurant and answer the questions.*

LA BAMBA RESTAURANT
Weekly Lunch Special

$25, served from 11:30 a.m. – 2:30 p.m.

Salad	Soup	Entrées	Drinks
• Caesar salad	• French onion	(All entrées come with a salad or soup)	• Coffee
• Chef salad	• Clam chowder	• Spaghetti	• Orange juice
		• Steak	• Black tea
		• Fish and chips	

① Which would you choose, a salad or soup?

   _____

② What would you like to order for the main course?

   _____

③ What would you like to order for your drink?

   _____

④ What do you think of the price? Do you think it's reasonable?

   _____

⑤ Would you like to try this restaurant? If yes, who would you go with?

   _____

CHALLENGE YOURSELF

Part I Pictures 🔘 1-13

Look at the picture and choose the best answer.

1.

☐ a   ☐ b   ☐ c

2.

☐ a   ☐ b   ☐ c

Part II Question & Response 🔘 1-14

Listen to the statement or question and choose the best response.

3. ☐ a   ☐ b   ☐ c   5. ☐ a   ☐ b   ☐ c
4. ☐ a   ☐ b   ☐ c   6. ☐ a   ☐ b   ☐ c

Part III Conversations 🔘 1-15

Listen to the conversation and answer the questions.

7. Why does Phil think it's OK to smoke?
   ☐ a. Nobody thinks it's rude.
   ☐ b. It's actually legal.
   ☐ c. The restroom is empty.

8. Where does Tim live?
   ☐ a. Nearby
   ☐ b. Pretty far away
   ☐ c. In another city

9. Is Dan going to go to the party?
   ☐ a. Absolutely.
   ☐ b. Maybe.
   ☐ c. Certainly not.

10. What kind of soup will he have?
    ☐ a. A kind with chicken
    ☐ b. A kind with beef
    ☐ c. A kind with seafood

Linguaporta Training

Let's review the unit with Linguaporta.

29

UNIT 03

Sports

WARM UP

TALK ABOUT THIS

Talk about these questions.

Do you prefer to watch sports or play sports?

ACTIVATE

A *Listen to the conversations and choose the correct pictures.* 🎧 1-16

Question 1.	Question 2.

What's the most popular sport in your country?

Question 3.

B *Role-play with a partner. Extend the conversation as much as you can.*

Ⓐ How often do you _____?

Ⓑ I _____ once a week.

⋯⋯⋯⋯⋯⋯⋯⋯⋯⋯⋯⋯⋯⋯⋯⋯⋯⋯⋯⋯⋯

Ⓐ How do I sign up for _____ classes?

Ⓑ We need your ID, and we'll issue you a membership card.

Staying in Shape

A *Watch the video clip and check the correct answers.* 📺

1. What do we know about Kurt?
   - [ ] **a.** He has little free time.
   - [ ] **b.** He goes jogging every day.
   - [ ] **c.** He has never been to Central Park.

2. What is something that Dana and Kurt have in common?
   - [ ] **a.** They both use apps when they exercise.
   - [ ] **b.** They both enjoy jogging.
   - [ ] **c.** They both live in the heart of town.

3. How often does Kurt go jogging?
   - [ ] **a.** At least a couple of times a day
   - [ ] **b.** At least a couple of times a month
   - [ ] **c.** At least a couple of times a week

4. Which of the following is true?
   - [ ] **a.** Kurt tracks his progress when jogging.
   - [ ] **b.** Dana never exercises.
   - [ ] **c.** Kurt and Dana work for different companies.

B *Listen to the conversation and fill in the blanks.* 🎧 1-17 🖥

Dana and Kurt are chatting. Dana asks Kurt about his hobbies.

Dana: So, what do you like to do in your free time, Kurt?

Kurt: To be ¹_____, I don't have much free time these days, but when I do, I try to get some exercise in.

Dana: Is there any ²_____ type of exercise that you prefer?

Kurt: Actually, jogging is my favorite. I try to jog at ³_____ a couple of times a week.

Dana: Really? I love to jog! Do you have a set route that you like to take?

Kurt: I usually go jogging at Central Park. It's really nice, not to ⁴_____ that it's right in the heart of town.

Dana: Is that so? Maybe I should go for a ⁵_____ there sometime, too.

Kurt: I recommend it! Another thing I like to do is use an app to ⁶_____ my progress.

Dana: Oh, I've ⁷_____ about those. Are they useful?

Kurt: I think so. I use one just about every time I go running. It's a convenient way to see how you're ⁸_____.

C *Practice the conversation with your partner.*

D *Listen to the short talk. Check how often the following sports are played on TV.* 🎧 1-18

☐ twice a week
☐ twice a month

☐ once a week
☐ once a month

☐ once a week
☐ four times a week

☐ twice a week
☐ twice a month

☐ twice a month
☐ four times a month

1 Adverbs of Frequency

$$S. + be + \begin{cases} \text{always} \\ \text{often} \\ \text{seldom} \end{cases} \quad \vdots \quad S. + \begin{cases} \text{always} \\ \text{often} \\ \text{seldom} \end{cases} + V.$$

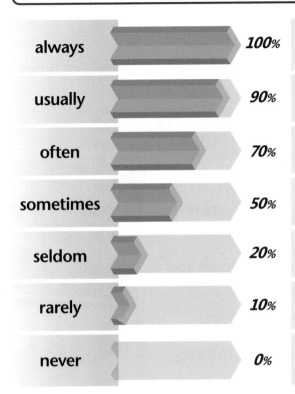

always	**100%**	• He's **always** late for class. ↳*after the be verb*
usually	**90%**	• It's not **usually** cold at night.
often	**70%**	• She **often** plays basketball. ↳*before the regular verb*
sometimes	**50%**	• They **sometimes** eat pasta for dinner.
seldom	**20%**	• I **seldom** take the bus to school.
rarely	**10%**	• It **rarely** rains in this country.
never	**0%**	• The kids are **never** afraid.

Work It Out

A *Check the correct answers.*

① I (☐ go usually / ☐ usually go) jogging at night.

② Lily (☐ never is / ☐ is never) late for school.

③ We (☐ sometimes go / ☐ go sometimes) to the movies on the weekend.

④ My dogs (☐ always are / ☐ are always) happy to see me.

⑤ My father (☐ seldom exercises / ☐ exercises seldom) in the morning.

B *Check the correct answers.*

My grandparents (☐ go always / ☐ always go) jogging in the morning. They (☐ often get / ☐ get often) up at six o'clock. It's (☐ usually sunny / ☐ sunny usually) where they live, so they (☐ never stop / ☐ stop never) exercising.

GRAMMAR   **2 Phrases of Frequency**

Adverbial Phrases

all the time		• I don't go bowling **all the time**.
every (other)	day / week / month	• Melody gets up early **every day**. • We go to the movies **every other week**.
once twice three times four times	a day / a week a month / a year	• My father goes jogging **once a day**. • Sean plays video games **twice a week**.
every other day every five days		• We play basketball **every other day**. • I go to the supermarket **every five days**.

How often

> **How often +** $\left\{ \begin{array}{c} \text{do} \\ \text{does} \end{array} \right\}$ **+ S. + V. ?**

• *A:* <u>How often</u> do you play baseball?

    ↳ *use **how often** to ask frequency*

    B: I play baseball **once a week / twice a week / three times a month**.

Work It Out

Ⓐ *What is true for you? Complete the sentences. Use a different adverbial phrase of frequency for each sentence.*

① I watch TV _____.   ④ I go out with friends _____.

② I sing karaoke _____.   ⑤ I play sports _____.

③ I eat instant noodles _____.

Ⓑ *Look at the pictures and write sentences using **how often**.*

① How often do Tracy and Lily go shopping? _____

    (Tracy and Lily)

② _____

    (Jay)

③ _____

    (Kitty and Anita) 35

Themed Races: Run for Fun

🎧 1-19

   Competitive running used to be considered a serious event. Now, a new generation of races has popped up around the world, using colors, food, and other themes to get people to run and stay fit.

   Among the most popular is the Color Run. Participants in this five-kilometer run
5 get sprayed from head to toe with colored powder after each kilometer. The event is a celebration of healthiness and happiness. Since it began in the U.S. in 2012, the Color Run has often held events in South America, Europe, and Asia.

   While the Color Run spreads happiness, fear is in the air at Run for Your Lives events. Here, racers must climb hills and cross muddy grounds and water to get
10 to the finish line—all the while being chased by hungry zombies. After the race, runners and zombie players can relax at the post-race party.

   An event that is much less terrifying is Canada's Chocolate Race. Participants receive chocolate-covered strawberries during the race and chocolate milk at the finish line. Then, everyone heads over to the park where other
15 chocolate-based foods are served.

   These and many other themed races have turned running into a creative activity, and it seems like every year a fun new event is being created. As a result, more and more people are becoming interested in running and maintaining a
20 healthy life.

A *Fill in the blanks with the word choices given. Change the word form if necessary.*

fit / terrifying / participant / result / maintain

1. Ken missed the bus. As a _____, he was late for school.

2. _____ were asked to fill out a questionnaire.

3. A large house is really expensive to _____.

4. Jill wants to get _____, so she will exercise more.

5. It was a _____ experience. I was so scared.

B *Check the correct answers.*

1. How long is the Color Run?
   ☐ a. Five kilometers
   ☐ b. Ten kilometers
   ☐ c. Fifteen kilometers

2. Where did the Color Run first begin?
   ☐ a. South America
   ☐ b. Europe
   ☐ c. The United States

3. What is found in the Run for Your Lives race?
   ☐ a. Color powder
   ☐ b. Muddy water
   ☐ c. Chocolate milk

4. Which event doesn't have an after-party?
   ☐ a. The Color Run
   ☐ b. Run for Your Lives
   ☐ c. The Chocolate Race

5. What can we infer from the article?
   ☐ a. Themed races have existed for many decades.
   ☐ b. Themed races are becoming more popular.
   ☐ c. Themed races are very serious, competitive events.

Have you ever participated in a sports competition? Write your answers. Then, discuss with your classmates.

Competition	When	Result
Baseball tournament	July 2020	Fourth place

37

WRITING

A *Look at the chart and answer the questions.*

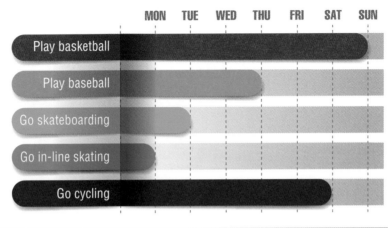

On the first day back to school, we interviewed 80 students about sports they played during summer vacation. Here are the results:

	MON	TUE	WED	THU	FRI	SAT	SUN
Play basketball							
Play baseball							
Go skateboarding							
Go in-line skating							
Go cycling							

① How often did they play basketball?

_____

② Did they play baseball every day?

_____

③ Did they often go in-line skating?

_____

④ How often did they go skateboarding?

_____

B *Use adverbs of frequency to write a paragraph about what you usually do in your free time.*

CHALLENGE YOURSELF

Part I Pictures 🎧 1-20

Look at the picture and choose the best answer.

1.

☐ a   ☐ b   ☐ c

2.

☐ a   ☐ b   ☐ c

Part II Question & Response 🎧 1-21

Listen to the statement or question and choose the best response.

3. ☐ a   ☐ b   ☐ c   5. ☐ a   ☐ b   ☐ c
4. ☐ a   ☐ b   ☐ c   6. ☐ a   ☐ b   ☐ c

Part III Conversations 🎧 1-22

Listen to the conversation and answer the questions.

7. What does the woman say about skiing?
   ☐ a. She likes it a lot.
   ☐ b. She doesn't do it often.
   ☐ c. She's too afraid to try it.

8. What does the man say about Mike?
   ☐ a. He's a good manager.
   ☐ b. He's a competent player.
   ☐ c. He needs more practice.

9. How often do they practice?
   ☐ a. Three times a month
   ☐ b. Once a week
   ☐ c. About every other day

10. What happened to Patrick?
   ☐ a. He lost his bike.
   ☐ b. He hurt his leg.
   ☐ c. He hurt his hand.

Linguaporta Training

Let's review the unit with Linguaporta.

39

WARM UP

TALK ABOUT THIS

Talk about these questions.

What do you do when you get a cold?

ACTIVATE

A *Listen to the conversations and choose the correct pictures.* 🎧 1-23

Question 1.

Question 2.

Are there any ways to prevent getting sick?

B *Role-play with a partner. Extend the conversation as much as you can.*

(A) You look sick. Are you all right?

(B) • I have a(n) _____.

• I feel _____.

(A) When did the problem start?

(B) It started _____.

(A) How long have you felt this way?

(B) The _____ has been on and off for a week.

Question 3.

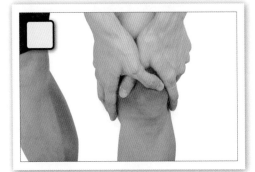

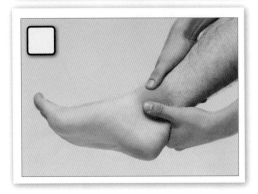

41

Seeing a Doctor

A *Watch the video clip and check the correct answers.* WEB動画

1. What did the doctor ask Kathy about after he took her temperature?
   ☐ **a.** Her job and social life
   ☐ **b.** Her last checkup
   ☐ **c.** Her eating and sleeping habits

2. Which body part was NOT checked by the doctor?
   ☐ **a.** Chest
   ☐ **b.** Throat
   ☐ **c.** Ear

3. What is wrong with Kathy, according to the doctor?
   ☐ **a.** She needs to go on a diet.
   ☐ **b.** She sleeps too much.
   ☐ **c.** She has the flu.

4. How many pills should Kathy take a day?
   ☐ **a.** One
   ☐ **b.** Two
   ☐ **c.** Three

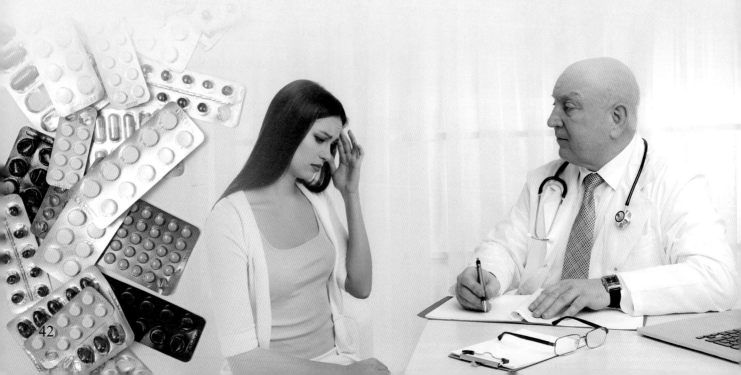

B *Listen to the conversation and fill in the blanks.* 🎧 1-24 💻

Kathy is not feeling well, so she has made an appointment to see her doctor.

Doctor: Come on in, Kathy. What seems to be the problem today?

Kathy: Well, I feel a bit under the ¹_____.

Doctor: Can you be more ²_____ about your symptoms?

Kathy: Yes. I have a headache, a sore throat, and I'm tired all the time.

Doctor: Those sound like ³_____ flu symptoms. Let me take a look at your throat. Please open your mouth and say "Ah."

Kathy: Ahhhh.

Doctor: Your throat is red. Now, let's take your temperature. Well, you have a ⁴_____ fever. Are you eating well and getting enough rest?

Kathy: Not really. Midterm exams are around the ⁵_____. That means I'm not getting enough sleep. I've been studying a lot lately and haven't been sleeping much. Also, sometimes, I forget to eat lunch and end up grabbing a snack from the convenience store.

Doctor: You're simply exhausted, with a ⁶_____ of the flu. Get some rest and drink enough water.

Kathy: Is that all, Doctor?

Doctor: Let me listen to your ⁷_____. Take some deep breaths. Your ⁸_____ sound clear. Here's a prescription. Take one pill in the morning and one in the evening. Come see me again in a week if you're still not feeling well.

Kathy: Thanks so much, Doc!

C *Practice the conversation with your partner.*

D *Listen and number the pictures 1 to 5.* 🎧 1-25

Infinitives (to V.)

- **To learn** a second language **is** challenging.
  - S.
  - → *singular verb*
- I want <u>to learn a second language</u>.
  - → *used as an object*

Gerunds (V-ing)

- <u>Going shopping</u> **is** my favorite leisure activity.
  - S.
  - → *singular verb*
- She enjoys <u>going shopping</u>.
  - → *used as an object*

Verbs followed by an infinitive

agree	ask	continue
decide	expect	hope
plan	promise	want

- Audrey wants to go on a vacation.
- My mom needs to buy some groceries.

Verbs followed by a gerund

avoid	can't help	deny
enjoy	mind	practice
quit		

- I enjoy watching TV after school.

Verbs followed by an infinitive or a gerund

begin	hate	like
love	start	

- I love reading.
- = I love to read.

False Subject

$$\text{It is } + \left\{ \begin{matrix} \textbf{adj.} \\ \textbf{N.} \end{matrix} \right\} + \textbf{(for sb) + to V.}$$

- <u>To win the lottery</u> is exciting. = It is exciting <u>to win the lottery</u>.
  - → *false subject*   → *real subject*

- <u>Exercising regularly</u> is good for your health. = It is <u>good</u> for your health <u>to exercise regularly</u>.
  - *false subject* ←┘   └→ *adj.*   └→ *real subject*

- <u>It</u> is a good <u>idea</u> <u>to learn about the culture of a country before visiting</u>.
  - └→ *false subject*   └→ *N.*   └→ *real subject*

Work It Out

A *Change to V. to V-ing; change V-ing to to V.*

① To see is to believe.

_____

② I started to get a cold last week.

_____

③ Kids hate going to the hospital.

_____

④ Sean loves to play the guitar.

_____

UNIT
04

HEALTH

B *Rewrite the following sentences using **It is … to …***

① To visit you is a pleasure.

_____

② To study English well is not hard.

_____

③ Watching TV is fun.

_____

④ To have good eating habits is important.

_____

GRAMMAR   **2 Stop/Remember/Forget + to V./V-ing**

stop	to V.	The bus **stopped to pick up** the children. → *tells us why something has stopped*
	V-ing	I've **stopped playing** baseball every weekend. → *tells us what has happened*
remember	to V.	Did you **remember to go** to the store? → *you have a chore or duty*
	V-ing	I'll always **remember traveling** to Germany. → *you remember something you did in the past*
forget	to V.	Don't **forget to send** me an e-mail. → *you have a chore or duty*
	V-ing	I'll never **forget meeting** you for the first time. → *you remember something you did in the past*

Work It Out

A *Fill in the blanks based on the hints given.*

① Don't forget _____ (turn) off the lights before you go to bed.

② I'll always remember _____ (fly) for the first time.

③ My father finally stopped _____ (eat) fast food every day.

④ Tony, remember _____ (finish) your homework this weekend.

⑤ Ken was lost, so he stopped _____ (ask) someone for help.

⑥ David never forgot _____ (meet) his favorite baseball player.

Health Threats Caused by Electronic Devices

🎧 1-26

How much time do you spend looking at your smartphone, tablet, or computer every day? These electronic devices help us in many ways, but they may also cause various health problems. Staring at electronic screens for too long can cause eyestrain. Not only will this leave your eyes feeling dry and sore, but it could also
5 affect your vision. In serious cases, eyestrain can finally lead to blindness and the need for surgery. To help your eyes stay healthy, follow the "20-20-20" rule. Every twenty minutes, focus on something twenty feet away for twenty seconds. This simple solution could save your sight.

Scientific research suggests that electronic devices can hurt your mind just as
10 much as your body. One of the biggest problems is that using these devices can affect your sleep patterns. Doctors say the light-emitting screens make you stop feeling sleepy. Therefore, they advise people not to use electronic devices for at least one hour before trying to sleep.

Another notable danger is Internet addiction. Experts say that many people
15 turn to the Internet to ease feelings of stress, sadness, and loneliness. Over time, they might start to rely on the Internet, thus becoming isolated from friends and family. To stop yourself from falling into this kind of trap, limit the amount of time you spend online. Remember—there is more to life than
20 looking at an electronic screen!

A *Fill in the blanks with the word choices given. Change the word form if necessary.*

> stare / affect / notable / surgery / device

1. This _____ separates metal from garbage.

2. How will the new road _____ the community?

3. "Hamlet" and "Macbeth" are among Shakespeare's most _____ works.

4. Betty screamed and everyone in the room turned to _____ at her.

5. The patient underwent _____ on her leg.

B *Check the correct answers.*

1. What is the article mainly about?
   - ☐ **a.** How to sleep better at night
   - ☐ **b.** How the Internet has improved society
   - ☐ **c.** How electronic devices can affect our health

2. How often should you focus on something 20 feet away?
   - ☐ **a.** Every 10 minutes
   - ☐ **b.** Every 15 minutes
   - ☐ **c.** Every 20 minutes

3. How can you stop yourself from falling into the trap of Internet addiction?
   - ☐ **a.** By restricting the amount of time spent online
   - ☐ **b.** By reducing the number of websites visited
   - ☐ **c.** By increasing the time spent on watching TV

4. How long before bed should you quit using electronic devices?
   - ☐ **a.** One hour
   - ☐ **b.** One minute
   - ☐ **c.** Twenty minutes

5. According to the article, people use the Internet to cope with which feeling?
   - ☐ **a.** Satisfaction
   - ☐ **b.** Anger
   - ☐ **c.** Loneliness

How long do you use these electronic devices every day? Which of the following electronic devices do you use most often? Rank them, with 1 being the electronic device you use the most often and 5 being the one you use the least often.

WRITING

Ⓐ *Read the patient information form and answer the questions.*

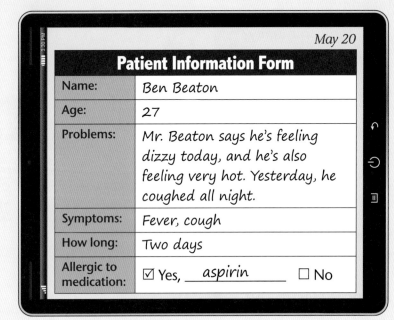

May 20

Patient Information Form

Name:	Ben Beaton
Age:	27
Problems:	Mr. Beaton says he's feeling dizzy today, and he's also feeling very hot. Yesterday, he coughed all night.
Symptoms:	Fever, cough
How long:	Two days
Allergic to medication:	☑ Yes, _aspirin_ ☐ No

① How is Ben feeling today?
_____
_____

② What are Ben's symptoms?
_____
_____

③ When did his problems start?
_____
_____

④ Is Ben allergic to any forms of medication?
_____
_____

Ⓑ *Rewrite the example paragraph below. Change the bold words and write your own paragraph.*

From	James <james.brown@liveabc.com>
To	Ms. Smith <dianasmith@mail.hebron.edu.tw>
Subject	I'm sick ...

*Dear **Ms. Smith,***

*I'm sick today. I'm feeling **hot**, and I think I **have a fever**. **I have a headache and sore throat**, too. **My roommate will take me to see a doctor**. So I want to take sick leave today. Thank you!*

Sincerely,
James

_____
_____
_____
_____
_____
_____

CHALLENGE YOURSELF

Part I Pictures 🎧 1-27

Look at the picture and choose the best answer.

1.

☐ a ☐ b ☐ c

2.

☐ a ☐ b ☐ c

Part II Question & Response 🎧 1-28

Listen to the statement or question and choose the best response.

3. ☐ a ☐ b ☐ c   5. ☐ a ☐ b ☐ c
4. ☐ a ☐ b ☐ c   6. ☐ a ☐ b ☐ c

Part III Conversations 🎧 1-29

Listen to the conversation and answer the questions.

7. What is likely true about Jimmy?
   ☐ a. He's feeling sick.
   ☐ b. His head hurts.
   ☐ c. He hurt his back.

8. Why are Dirk's eyes red?
   ☐ a. Someone is irritating him.
   ☐ b. They're sensitive to dirt.
   ☐ c. He's a little tired out now.

9. What is wrong with Carla?
   ☐ a. She has a pain in her stomach.
   ☐ b. She has a pain in her back.
   ☐ c. She's unable to stand steadily.

10. What is Dana suffering from?
    ☐ a. A stomachache
    ☐ b. A fever
    ☐ c. A headache

Linguaporta Training

Let's review the unit with Linguaporta.

What's on Your Playlist?

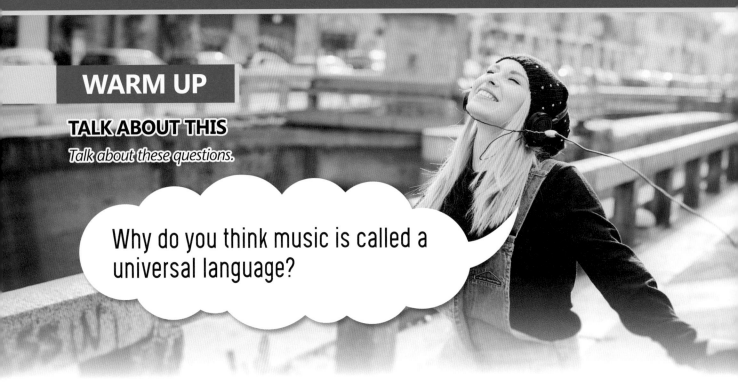

WARM UP

TALK ABOUT THIS

Talk about these questions.

Why do you think music is called a universal language?

ACTIVATE

A *Listen to the conversations and choose the correct pictures.* 🎵 1-30

Question 1.

Question 2.

Can you play any musical instruments?

B *Role-play with a partner. Extend the conversation as much as you can.*

Ⓐ Are you good at music?

Ⓑ Yes, I can play the _____.

....

Ⓐ Can you play the _____?

Ⓑ • Yes, I can.
   • No, I can't.

Question 3.

51

CONVERSATION

Sounds Like a Good Hobby

A *Watch the video clip and check the correct answers.* WEB動画

1. What instrument does Stuart play?
   - ☐ **a.** Guitar
   - ☐ **b.** Piano
   - ☐ **c.** Violin

2. What type of music does Ryan like?
   - ☐ **a.** Classical music
   - ☐ **b.** Rock music
   - ☐ **c.** Pop music

3. Why doesn't Ryan choose drums?
   - ☐ **a.** Because they're too heavy.
   - ☐ **b.** Because they're too light.
   - ☐ **c.** Because they're too loud.

4. What will Ryan probably do next?
   - ☐ **a.** Buy a new guitar
   - ☐ **b.** Buy a secondhand violin
   - ☐ **c.** Join Stuart's band

Stuart

Ryan

52

B *Listen to the conversation and fill in the blanks.* 🎧 1-31 📺

Stuart: I'm going over to a friend's house. We're in a band together.

Ryan: Cool! What [1]_____ do you play?

Stuart: I play the guitar. I love classical music. Are you interested in music?

Ryan: I'm a big fan of rock music, but I don't know how to play anything. [2]_____ I just listen to my favorite groups and sometimes go to concerts.

Stuart: Music's a great hobby. If you like rock and roll, the drums would be perfect for you.

Ryan: I don't know. Drums are noisy. They will probably make my [3]_____ mad.

Stuart: OK. [4]_____ instruments could be just the thing for you. They're small and light. They're not too [5]_____, so you won't bother your neighbors.

Ryan: What [6]_____ do I have?

Stuart: How about a violin? You could also try the bass or the cello.

Ryan: Oh, I like the violin. They sound beautiful, and they look nice, too.

Stuart: Sure, violins are a very [7]_____ instrument.

Ryan: But aren't violins expensive?

Stuart: They're not cheap, but you can get a [8]_____ violin.

Ryan: Good idea! I'll go to the music store and pick one up.

C *Practice the conversation with your partner.*

D *Hi. I'm Hannah! Listen to the conversation and circle the details about me.* 🎧 1-32

Musical Instruments	Favorite Type of Music	Favorite Singer
piano	hip-hop	DJ Johnny
violin	jazz	
viola	classical	Lilly Tyler
saxophone	country	
guitar	blues	Norah Jones
cello	rock	

GRAMMAR   Correlative Conjunctions

Correlative conjunctions work in pairs to connect phrases or words that carry two equal grammatical structures.

both ... and

- The research project will take **both** <u>time</u> **and** <u>money</u>.
  ⤷ *to join similar words*

- **Both** <u>Sid</u> **and** <u>Nathan</u> **want** to ride in the
  connected with plural verb
  front seat.

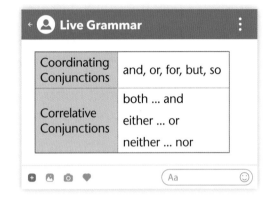

Live Grammar

Coordinating Conjunctions	and, or, for, but, so
Correlative Conjunctions	both ... and
	either ... or
	neither ... nor

Aa

not only ... but (also)

- Megan is **not only** <u>creative</u> **but (also)** <u>funny</u>.
  ⤷ *to join similar words*

- **Not only** <u>Craig</u> **but (also)** <u>his parents</u> **live** in France.
  ⤷ *verb agrees with the subject closest to the verb*

either ... or / neither ... nor

- Most of the food at the restaurant was **either** <u>too salty</u> **or** <u>too sweet</u>.
  ⤷ *to join similar words*

- **Either** <u>Thomas</u> **or** <u>I</u> **am** going to call you tomorrow about the job.
  ⤷ *verb agrees with the subject closest to the verb*

- Bernard can play **neither** <u>guitar</u> **nor** <u>piano</u>.
  ⤷ *to join similar words*

- **Neither** <u>Rita</u> **nor** <u>I</u> **know** how to change the tire on the car.
  ⤷ *verb agrees with the subject closest to the verb*

Work It Out

A *Fill in the blanks with correlative conjunctions.*

① The child wants neither cheesecake _____ ice cream.

② Benjamin can _____ play basketball and in-line skate well.

③ We'll go to _____ Prague Square or Charles Bridge.

④ I like to watch both action movies _____ romances.

⑤ She has _____ a desktop nor a laptop.

B *Read the passage and fill in the blanks with correlative conjunctions.*

My best friend Janet and I have a lot in common. _____ she and I like to eat pasta. We eat _____ pizza nor hamburgers. We like to either sing karaoke _____ go to the movies in our leisure time. We always choose _____ a comedy or horror movie to see at the movie theater. We really want to go to _____ Central Park and Times Square during our summer vacation. Because we have so much in common, we've decided to become roommates.

C *Check the correct answers.*

① Either my father or my mother (☐ is / ☐ are) going to the supermarket.

② Neither the webcam nor the speakers (☐ is / ☐ are) broken.

③ Neither Sarah nor I (☐ want / ☐ wants) to go shopping with them.

④ Both Spanish and German (☐ are / ☐ is) taught in this high school.

⑤ Either Sam or his friend (☐ have / ☐ has) eaten the cake.

D *Combine the sentences based on the hints given.*

① My roommate doesn't have a notebook. / I don't have a notebook. (neither ... nor ...)

_____

② Tom Hanks may be the leading actor of the movie. / Tom Cruise may be the leading actor of the movie. (either ... or ...)

_____

③ Paul invited me out for dinner tonight. / Peter also invited me out for dinner tonight. (both ... and ...)

_____

The Beautiful Guitar

🎵 1-33

The great musician and composer Frederic Chopin once said, "Nothing is more beautiful than a guitar, save perhaps two." It seems that many people agree with him, because the guitar is one of the world's most popular musical instruments. The modern electric guitar became popular in the 1950s and 1960s. The guitar

5 has a long history. The name comes from two Sanskrit words: char and tar, which mean "four" and "string." Nowadays, it is rare to see a new rock or pop band that doesn't include at least one electric guitar.

Not all guitars are considered equal, and some were sold for <u>jaw-dropping</u> prices. Famous guitarist Eric Clapton played one in concert and sold the guitar for

10 nearly US$1 million to raise money for poor people. But if you want to learn the guitar, don't worry—you can find guitars that are suitable for almost any budget.

Learning a musical instrument takes not only time but also effort. But it's worth it! As guitarist Jimi Hendrix said, "Sometimes you want to give up the

15 guitar—you'll hate the guitar—but if you stick with it, you're going to be rewarded." So don't let either price or difficulty discourage you. You might just be the next world-famous guitarist!

A *Fill in the blanks with the word choices given. Change the word form if necessary.*

rare / equal / budget / nearly / effort

1. That car _____ hit you.

2. The school _____ is going to be cut again this year.

3. This museum is full of _____ and precious treasures.

4. Ben lifted the box easily, without using much _____ .

5. All people are _____ , deserving the same rights as each other.

B *Check the correct answers.*

1. Where does the word "guitar" come from?
   - ☐ **a.** A Sanskrit word meaning "beautiful"
   - ☐ **b.** Two words in another language
   - ☐ **c.** Words by Frederic Chopin

2. What does the underlined word "jaw-dropping" mean?
   - ☐ **a.** Surprising
   - ☐ **b.** Similar
   - ☐ **c.** Ordinary

3. What do we know about the guitar?
   - ☐ **a.** Frederic Chopin didn't like it.
   - ☐ **b.** It is a very rare instrument.
   - ☐ **c.** It is popular all around the world.

4. Which of the following statements is correct?
   - ☐ **a.** All rock or pop bands include a guitar.
   - ☐ **b.** All guitars are the exact same quality.
   - ☐ **c.** Guitars have a wide range of prices.

5. What can we infer about the guitar, according to Jimi Hendrix?
   - ☐ **a.** If you give it up easily, you will earn a lot of money.
   - ☐ **b.** If you continue to practice it, you might be a successful guitarist.
   - ☐ **c.** If you want to be a famous guitarist, you need an expensive guitar.

Have you ever learned any of the following instruments? Check and share your experience with your classmates.

☐  ☐  ☐  ☐  ☐  ☐

WRITING

A *Read the flyer and answer the questions in full sentences.*

Do you like to listen to music?
Then why not learn to play a musical instrument?
It doesn't cost a lot of money.

We have beginner lessons for
drums, flute, guitar, piano, and violin.

* Wagner's Music School is open from 10 a.m. to 8 p.m., Monday through Friday, and from 11 a.m. to 6 p.m. on weekends.

* Our phone number is 2876-3428.

① What kinds of music lessons does Wagner's Music School teach?

_____

② Does it cost a lot of money to learn to play a musical instrument?

_____

③ When is the school open on weekends?

_____

B *What do you think it's like to be a famous musician? Write a paragraph about your daily life if you were a pop star or rock star.*

First, I wake up at 3:00 p.m. I'm a rock star, so I stay up late and sleep late. Then, I make some coffee and practice the guitar. I tell my personal chef to prepare a nice breakfast for me. When I finally leave the house, there are paparazzi waiting outside! They try to take my picture, but I put my hood up and run past them.

CHALLENGE YOURSELF

Part I Pictures 🎧 1-34

Look at the picture and choose the best answer.

1.

☐ a   ☐ b   ☐ c

2.

☐ a   ☐ b   ☐ c

Part II Question & Response 🎧 1-35

Listen to the statement or question and choose the best response.

3. ☐ a   ☐ b   ☐ c   5. ☐ a   ☐ b   ☐ c
4. ☐ a   ☐ b   ☐ c   6. ☐ a   ☐ b   ☐ c

Part III Conversations 🎧 1-36

Listen to the conversation and answer the questions.

7. What is true about the girl?
   ☐ a. She no longer wants to play music.
   ☐ b. She wants a guitar and a violin.
   ☐ c. She used to want a guitar.

8. What does the woman mean?
   ☐ a. She's unfamiliar with the band.
   ☐ b. She's too old to listen to the band.
   ☐ c. She can't get in touch with the band.

9. What does the man say about the song?
   ☐ a. It's his favorite one.
   ☐ b. It's not right for the ad.
   ☐ c. They're not allowed to use it.

10. What does the man want the woman to try?
   ☐ a. A toothbrush that uses power
   ☐ b. A toothbrush that only dentists use
   ☐ c. A toothbrush that is very soft

Linguaporta Training

Let's review the unit with Linguaporta.

59

At the Movies

WARM UP

TALK ABOUT THIS
Talk about these questions.

What's your favorite movie?

ACTIVATE

A *Listen to the conversations and choose the correct pictures.* 🎧 1-37

Question 1.	Question 2.

Do you think being an actor is a hard or easy job?

Question 3.

B *Role-play with a partner. Extend the conversation as much as you can.*

Ⓐ Let's go to the movies. There is a(n) _____ coming out this week.

Ⓑ Sounds good, but I'd prefer a(n) _____.

Ⓐ Is it _____?

Ⓑ Yeah, it is.

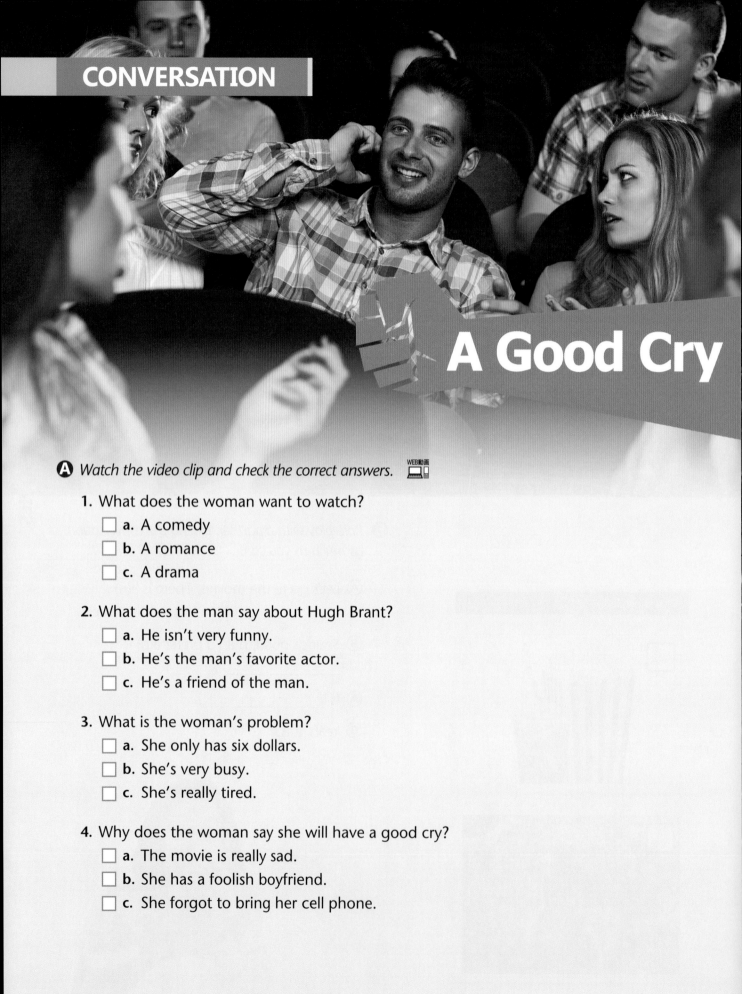

A Good Cry

A *Watch the video clip and check the correct answers.* WEB動画 🖥️📲

1. What does the woman want to watch?
   - ☐ **a.** A comedy
   - ☐ **b.** A romance
   - ☐ **c.** A drama

2. What does the man say about Hugh Brant?
   - ☐ **a.** He isn't very funny.
   - ☐ **b.** He's the man's favorite actor.
   - ☐ **c.** He's a friend of the man.

3. What is the woman's problem?
   - ☐ **a.** She only has six dollars.
   - ☐ **b.** She's very busy.
   - ☐ **c.** She's really tired.

4. Why does the woman say she will have a good cry?
   - ☐ **a.** The movie is really sad.
   - ☐ **b.** She has a foolish boyfriend.
   - ☐ **c.** She forgot to bring her cell phone.

B *Listen to the conversation and fill in the blanks.* 🎧 1-38 📺

Todd and Ashley are making plans for Saturday night.

Todd: I know! Let's go to the movies. A new comedy just came out. I just heard my friends talking about it. It sounds pretty good.

Ashley: I'd ¹_____ see a romance. Then I can have a good cry.

Todd: Well, how about a romantic comedy? I can laugh, and you can cry!

Ashley: OK. We could see *Wild Weekend Wedding*. It ²_____ Hugh Brant and Peg Ryan.

Todd: Great. Hugh Brant is my favorite actor. Where is it playing?

Ashley: It just opened, so it's playing everywhere. There's a ³_____, though. I only have six dollars.

Todd: I'll tell you ⁴_____. I'll buy the tickets if you buy the popcorn.

Todd and Ashley are in the theater. Todd is laughing his head off.

Ashley: Todd! Shh! Don't laugh so loud. You're ⁵_____ me.

Todd: I can't ⁶_____ it. Hugh Brant is so funny! Ha ha ha! I forgot to turn off my cell phone. Isn't that a great ringtone, though?

Ashley: Oh, Todd! You're ⁷_____ the movie for everyone.

Todd: I'm sorry. I'll turn off my phone. Ha ha ha! Someone just pushed Hugh Brant into the pool! Ha ha ha!

Ashley: I guess I'll have a good cry after all. I'll cry because I have a ⁸_____ for a boyfriend.

C *Practice the conversation with your partner.*

D *Listen to the short talk and complete the chart.* 🎧 1-39

Vince Vaughn	Nicole Kidman	Reese Witherspoon
Robert Downey Jr.	Hugh Jackman	Gwyneth Paltrow

Movie Title	Type of Movie	Leading Actor	Leading Actress
Australia			
Four Christmases			
Iron Man			

GRAMMAR

1 Sense Verbs

A **sense verb** is a verb that describes one of the five senses: sight, sound, smell, touch, and taste.

$$S. + \begin{Bmatrix} see \\ watch \\ hear \\ feel \end{Bmatrix} + O. + \begin{Bmatrix} V. \\ V\text{-ing} \\ P.P. \end{Bmatrix}$$

- I **saw** him <u>dance</u> in the park.
  ↳ use base verb to emphasize a fact

- I can **hear** the dog <u>barking</u>.
  ↳ use V-ing to emphasize an action

- Polly **felt** <u>unloved</u> by her parents.
  ↳ use p.p. to show passive meaning

There are verbs that can exist as action verbs or linking verbs. They are related to the five sense verbs.

$$\begin{Bmatrix} look \\ taste \\ sound \\ feel \\ smell \end{Bmatrix} + \begin{Bmatrix} like\ N. \\ adj. \end{Bmatrix}$$

- Kevin's eyes **look** <u>like his father's eyes</u>.
  ↳ to compare the similarity between two nouns

- The soup **tasted** <u>great</u> and I had another bowl.
  ↳ to describe personal thoughts about things

Work It Out

Ⓐ *Write a new sentence using sense verbs.*

① Someone was singing in the classroom. (Nancy heard it.)

_____

② A strange man was entering the room. (Did you notice it?)

_____

③ Something was burning in the kitchen. (Joe smelled it.)

_____

64

GRAMMAR   **2 Reflexive Pronouns**

*Reflexive pronouns end in **-self** or **-selves**. They are used when the subject and the object of a sentence are the same.*

Singular

Subject	Reflexive Pronoun
I	myself
you	yourself
he	himself
she	herself
it	itself

Plural

Subject	Reflexive Pronoun
we	ourselves
you	yourselves
they	themselves

• He cut **himself** by accident.
  → *the subject and the object are the same*

• We **ourselves** did it.
  → *used for emphasis*

• Jill painted this picture **by herself**.

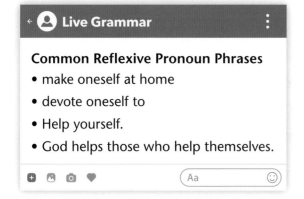

← 👤 **Live Grammar**   ⋮

Common Reflexive Pronoun Phrases
• make oneself at home
• devote oneself to
• Help yourself.
• God helps those who help themselves.

➕ 🖼 📷 ♥   (Aa   ☺)

Work It Out

A *Fill in the blanks with reflexive pronouns.*

① Did you make the dress by _____?

② Bruce wrote this song _____.

③ I hurt _____ while I was jogging.

④ Ellen bought a gift for _____ at the department store.

⑤ I'd like to design a house by _____ one day.

How Horror Hooks and Helps Us

🎧 1-40

Most of us avoid fearful situations. When we do find ourselves in such situations, our immediate reaction may be to run away. If this is the case, then why do so many people seek out the feeling of fear by watching horror movies? When we watch horror movies, we're satisfying an urge to sharpen our fear, just
5　as young animals play-fight to train themselves for real fights.

Watching horror films not only trains our minds to react to danger, but it may also be good for our health. When we're afraid, our blood flow and heart rate increase. This causes our bodies to release a substance called adrenaline. It lets our bodies burn more calories. One study even found that almost 200 extra
10　calories can be burned as a result of watching a heart-pounding scary movie. No doubt, fear can produce some positive psychological and physical effects on us. In this sense, horror films give us certain advantages, since they present danger on screen.

Of course, people with heart conditions and blood-pressure problems should
15　think carefully before putting themselves through any <u>hair-raising</u> experiences. For normal, healthy people, however, horror movies can be a safe place for some good fun.

A *Fill in the blanks with the word choices given. Change the word form if necessary.*

immediate / extra / substance / urge / scary

1. I have a(n) _____ ticket to the show.

2. I've always found Robert a bit _____.

3. Rubber is a flexible _____.

4. Ashley felt a(n) _____ to tell someone about what had happened.

5. The drug had a(n) _____ effect on the patient.

B *Check the correct answers.*

1. Which question best summarizes the topic of this passage?
   - ☐ a. What are the different kinds of horror movies?
   - ☐ b. When were horror movies invented?
   - ☐ c. Why do people like watching horror movies?

2. What is watching horror movies similar to, according to the article?
   - ☐ a. Play-fighting among young animals
   - ☐ b. Being attacked by a wild beast
   - ☐ c. Putting yourself into danger

3. What happens to our bodies when we're afraid, according to the article?
   - ☐ a. Our hearts beat faster.
   - ☐ b. We sweat a lot.
   - ☐ c. We can't fall asleep.

4. How many calories can be burned by watching a heart-pounding scary movie, according to the article?
   - ☐ a. 100 calories
   - ☐ b. Close to 200 calories
   - ☐ c. More than 200 calories

5. What does the underlined word "hair-raising" mean?
   - ☐ a. Very satisfying
   - ☐ b. Very interesting
   - ☐ c. Very frightening

WRITING

A *Read the timetable and answer the questions.*

Timetable			Ticket Price		
Movie	Time(s)	Day(s)	Adults	Students	Children under 12
Star Wars—sci-fi movie	7:00	Tues. / Thurs.	$12	$8	$5
Coco—animated movie	6:00 & 8:00	Mon. / Wed. / Fri.			
Get Out—horror movie	Midnight	Mon. only	(25% off on Tuesdays and Thursdays)		
La La Land—musical	2:30	Sat. / Sun.			

① Have you ever seen the above movies? Who went to the movie with you?

_____

② What kind of movies do you like?

_____

③ What is your favorite movie? Why?

_____

_____

B *Read the example paragraph below. Change the bold words and write your own paragraph.*

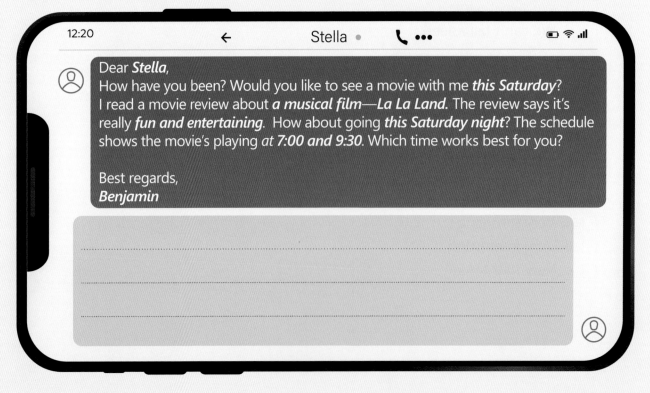

12:20   ←   Stella •   📞 •••

Dear **Stella**,
How have you been? Would you like to see a movie with me **this Saturday**?
I read a movie review about **a musical film—La La Land.** The review says it's really **fun and entertaining**. How about going **this Saturday night**? The schedule shows the movie's playing **at 7:00 and 9:30**. Which time works best for you?

Best regards,
Benjamin

CHALLENGE YOURSELF

Part I Pictures 🎧 1-41

Look at the picture and choose the best answer.

1.

☐ a   ☐ b   ☐ c

2.

☐ a   ☐ b   ☐ c

Part II Question & Response 🎧 1-42

Listen to the statement or question and choose the best response.

3. ☐ a   ☐ b   ☐ c   5. ☐ a   ☐ b   ☐ c
4. ☐ a   ☐ b   ☐ c   6. ☐ a   ☐ b   ☐ c

Part III Conversations 🎧 1-43

Listen to the conversation and answer the questions.

7. Which of the following statements is correct?
   ☐ a. She doesn't feel like watching the documentary.
   ☐ b. She really wants to watch the documentary.
   ☐ c. She says she really hates history.

8. What does the man think of the movie?
   ☐ a. It's fantastic.
   ☐ b. It's not so bad.
   ☐ c. It's really bad.

9. What kind of movie is the man probably watching?
   ☐ a. An action movie
   ☐ b. A horror movie
   ☐ c. A comedy

10. What is the woman suggesting?
   ☐ a. She wants to sell her ticket to the man.
   ☐ b. She doesn't like the movie.
   ☐ c. She wants to watch the movie, too.

Linguaporta Training

Let's review the unit with Linguaporta.

Part I 🎧 1-44

Listen to the statement or question and check the best response.

1. ☐ a ☐ b ☐ c   3. ☐ a ☐ b ☐ c
2. ☐ a ☐ b ☐ c   4. ☐ a ☐ b ☐ c

Part II 🎧 1-45

Listen to the conversation and check the correct answer.

1. Where is this conversation taking place?
   - ☐ a. At a bakery
   - ☐ b. At a doctor's office
   - ☐ c. At a film club

2. What does the boy want to do?
   - ☐ a. He wants to be more like his father.
   - ☐ b. He wants to have a life similar to his mother's.
   - ☐ c. He wants his mother to be proud of him.

3. Where are these people?
   - ☐ a. In a computer store
   - ☐ b. In a restaurant
   - ☐ c. In a supermarket

4. Which statement is true?
   - ☐ a. They will go skydiving first thing after lunch.
   - ☐ b. The hang-gliding activity has been canceled.
   - ☐ c. Jogging is not one of the planned activities.

Part III 🎧 1-46

Listen to the short passage and check the correct picture.

1.
 ☐ a    ☐ b    ☐ c

2.
 ☐ a    ☐ b    ☐ c

Part IV

Fill in the blanks.

> grilled / appointment / demand / sauce / goal / hill / prefers / fit /
> main course / under the weather

1. Carl _____ noodles to rice.

2. Luke's _____ was to start his own business.

3. The _____ for new cars has decreased in recent years.

4. The chef served _____ salmon filets with a mango and red onion salsa.

5. Holly likes to put cheese _____ on her vegetables.

6. "What will we have for the _____?" "How about steak? It's delicious."

7. That _____ is too steep to climb.

8. Bonnie goes running every day, so she's very _____.

9. Nelson just phoned to say he's feeling _____ and won't be in today.

10. Ryan has a(n) _____ with a dentist this Friday at 9:00 a.m.

Part V

Check the correct answer.

1. How _____ do you see your friends?
   - ☐ **a.** usually
   - ☐ **b.** often
   - ☐ **c.** sometimes
   - ☐ **d.** never

2. Beatrice's feet are _____ big to fit in those shoes.
   - ☐ **a.** too
   - ☐ **b.** enough
   - ☐ **c.** as
   - ☐ **d.** more

3. _____ Lucas didn't have time to change clothes before dinner, he still looked very nice.
   - ☐ **a.** Although
   - ☐ **b.** But
   - ☐ **c.** However
   - ☐ **d.** If

4. The doctor suggested that my father stop _____.
   - ☐ **a.** smoke
   - ☐ **b.** smoking
   - ☐ **c.** to smoke
   - ☐ **d.** smokes

5. Men tend to enjoy flipping through channels _____ women tend to stick to just one.
   - ☐ **a.** when
   - ☐ **b.** which
   - ☐ **c.** why
   - ☐ **d.** while

6. We saw some fish _____ in the river.
   - ☐ **a.** swims
   - ☐ **b.** swam
   - ☐ **c.** swimming
   - ☐ **d.** to swim

7. Either Bobby or I _____ take out the garbage tonight.
   - ☐ **a.** has to
   - ☐ **b.** have to
   - ☐ **c.** had
   - ☐ **d.** has

8. Would you mind if I _____ the window?
   - ☐ **a.** opening
   - ☐ **b.** am opening
   - ☐ **c.** will open
   - ☐ **d.** open

9. Don't forget _____ off the air conditioner before you go out.
   - ☐ **a.** turn
   - ☐ **b.** turning
   - ☐ **c.** to turn
   - ☐ **d.** to turning

10. God helps those who help _____.
    - ☐ **a.** they
    - ☐ **b.** their
    - ☐ **c.** them
    - ☐ **d.** themselves

71

Part VI 🎧 1-47

Read the article and check the correct answer.

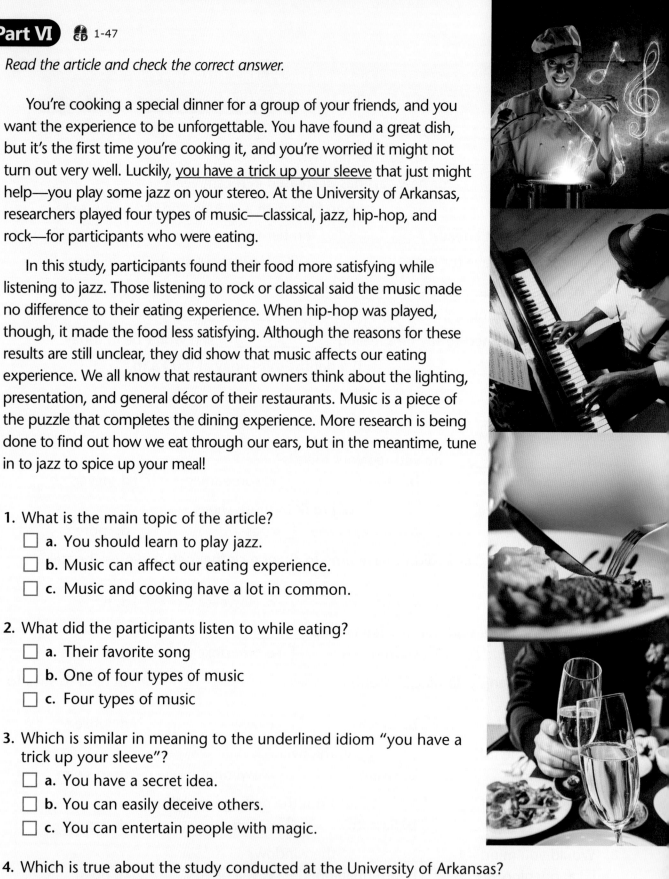

You're cooking a special dinner for a group of your friends, and you want the experience to be unforgettable. You have found a great dish, but it's the first time you're cooking it, and you're worried it might not turn out very well. Luckily, <u>you have a trick up your sleeve</u> that just might
5 help—you play some jazz on your stereo. At the University of Arkansas, researchers played four types of music—classical, jazz, hip-hop, and rock—for participants who were eating.

In this study, participants found their food more satisfying while listening to jazz. Those listening to rock or classical said the music made
10 no difference to their eating experience. When hip-hop was played, though, it made the food less satisfying. Although the reasons for these results are still unclear, they did show that music affects our eating experience. We all know that restaurant owners think about the lighting, presentation, and general décor of their restaurants. Music is a piece of
15 the puzzle that completes the dining experience. More research is being done to find out how we eat through our ears, but in the meantime, tune in to jazz to spice up your meal!

1. What is the main topic of the article?
   ☐ a. You should learn to play jazz.
   ☐ b. Music can affect our eating experience.
   ☐ c. Music and cooking have a lot in common.

2. What did the participants listen to while eating?
   ☐ a. Their favorite song
   ☐ b. One of four types of music
   ☐ c. Four types of music

3. Which is similar in meaning to the underlined idiom "you have a trick up your sleeve"?
   ☐ a. You have a secret idea.
   ☐ b. You can easily deceive others.
   ☐ c. You can entertain people with magic.

4. Which is true about the study conducted at the University of Arkansas?
   ☐ a. The participants found their food less satisfying while listening to rock.
   ☐ b. Hip-hop made no difference to the participants' eating experience.
   ☐ c. The reasons for the results are still unknown.

5. What is the best title for this passage?

☐ **a.** Four Popular Types of Music

☐ **b.** Music Makes Food Taste Better

☐ **c.** Different Tastes in Food and Music

Part VII

Answer the questions in full sentences with the hints given.

1. How often do you go traveling? *(three times a year)*

_____

2. Are your parents always busy with work? *(yes)*

_____

Complete the sentences based on your personal information.

1. I always _____

2. I usually _____

3. I sometimes _____

4. I seldom _____

5. I never _____

Answer the questions based on your personal information.

1. Do you prefer to watch sports or play sports?

_____

2. Can you play any musical instruments?

_____

3. What do you do when you get a cold?

_____

4. How are you going to spend your summer vacation?

_____

5. Have you ever been abroad? If yes, when and where?

_____

_____

WARM UP

TALK ABOUT THIS

Talk about these questions.

> Which appliance is least helpful?
>
> How can it be improved?

ACTIVATE

A *Listen to the conversations and choose the correct pictures.* 🎧 2-01

Question 1.	Question 2.

	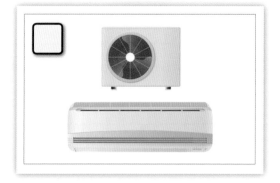

> Do you think TVs will eventually become obsolete?

UNIT
07

TECHNOLOGY IN DAILY LIFE

Question 3.

B *Role-play with a partner. Extend the conversation as much as you can.*

A Thanks so much for inviting me for lunch / dinner .

B You're welcome. I'm glad you could come.

....

A This is what we need for the bedroom / living room / dining room / kitchen .

B Agreed. Let's get it.

....

A Wouldn't a(n) _____ be better?

B I don't think so. It's too expensive. This one is much cheaper.

CONVERSATION

New Home, New Electronics

Ⓐ *Watch the video clip and check the correct answers.* 🖥️

1. Why are Elon and Betty shopping?
   - ☐ **a.** They need to buy a birthday present.
   - ☐ **b.** They need to buy things for their new house.
   - ☐ **c.** They need to replace their broken electronics.

2. What does Elon want to buy?
   - ☐ **a.** A home entertainment system
   - ☐ **b.** A vacuum cleaner
   - ☐ **c.** A stereo with speakers

3. What size screen would Betty prefer to buy?
   - ☐ **a.** Forty inches
   - ☐ **b.** Forty-five inches
   - ☐ **c.** Fifty-five inches

4. What is special about the clerk's suggested setup?
   - ☐ **a.** It has a low-definition display.
   - ☐ **b.** It comes with a free vacuum.
   - ☐ **c.** It has wireless connectivity.

B *Listen to the conversation and fill in the blanks.* 🎧 2-02 📺WEB動画

Elon and Betty are shopping in an electronics store. A clerk approaches them.

Clerk: Welcome to Electronics World. If you have any questions, I'd be happy to give you advice.

Elon: Thanks. Actually, we were looking to buy a home [1]_____ system for our new house.

Betty: That, along with some other items. We just moved into a new house, so we need to [2]_____ some of our old electronics.

Clerk: I'm here to help. We could start with the home [3]_____. Were you thinking about any particular brand, screen size, or sound system?

Elon: I don't know about brands, but I'd [4]_____ like something with a surround-sound stereo system.

Betty: As for size, I think a forty-inch screen would be about right; [5]_____, it'd be too big for our living room.

Clerk: Considering your needs, I'd suggest this setup—It comes with five speakers all wireless, [6]_____ to Bluetooth technology.

Betty: Is it easy to [7]_____?

Clerk: Yes, it is. You can also download the instructions on our website.

Betty: Uh, let's look at some other items before we decide on the home theater. First, I need a vacuum cleaner.

Clerk: Have you considered buying a Roomba? You'd never have to [8]_____ a finger to vacuum again.

Betty: A Roomba?

Clerk: It's a robotic vacuum cleaner. Let me show you.

C *Practice the conversation with your partner.*

D *Listen to the conversation and check what they want to buy.* 🎧 2-03

GRAMMAR   **1 Dative Case**

*The dative case shows the relationship of an indirect object
to a verb. An indirect object is the recipient of a direct object.
The indirect object receives the direct object.*

> **S. + Vt. + Indirect Object (I.O.) + Direct Object (D.O.)**
> **= S. + Vt. + D.O. + Prep. + I.O**

← 👤 Live Grammar   ⋮

Verbs	prep.
bring, give, lend, send, show, write	to
buy, find, get, leave, make, save	for
ask	of
borrow	from

➕ 🖼 📷 ♥   (Aa)   ☺

- Ryan **gave** Sophie the letter.
  ↳ I.O.   ↳ D.O.
- = Ryan **gave** the letter **to** Sophie.
  ↳ D.O. ↳ prep. ↳ I.O.

- If I get good grades this semester, my mother will **buy** me a new camera.
  ↳ I.O.   ↳ D.O.
- = If I get good grades this semester, my mother will **buy** a new camera **for** me.
  ↳ D.O.   prep. ↳ I.O.

Work It Out

Ⓐ *Complete the sentences.*

① May I ask you a favor?
= May I ask a favor _____ you?

② I bought a Christmas gift for her.
= I bought _____.

③ Dave borrowed 200 dollars _____ his girlfriend.

④ Will you buy me a pen?
= Will you buy a pen _____ me?

Ⓑ *Complete the following sentences based on the hints given.*

① You must give (the book / Tom).
  You must give the book to Tom.
  You must give Tom the book.

② Jenny and Linda got (presents / each other).
  _____
  _____

③ Julia made (some coffee / her guests).
  _____
  _____

78

2 Conjuctive Adverbs: However

A conjunctive adverb can join one clause to another. Like other adverbs, conjunctive adverbs may be moved around in the sentence or clause in which they appear.

- I'd like to help you; **however,** I think you'll learn more if you do it yourself.
  ↳ *used to link two independent main clauses*

- This coffee maker doesn't cost much. The quality, **however,** isn't very good.
  ↳ *in the middle of one independent clause*

- This smartphone is really nice. **However,** it's quite expensive.
  ↳ *used in a single main clause*

- Almost everyone felt sick after the boat ride. Evan felt great, **however.**
  ↳ *used in a single main clause*

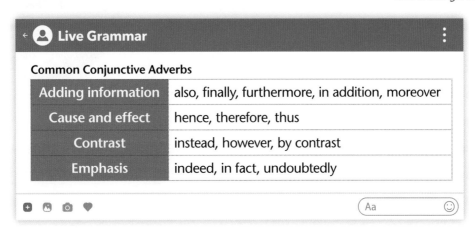

Live Grammar

Common Conjunctive Adverbs

Adding information	also, finally, furthermore, in addition, moreover
Cause and effect	hence, therefore, thus
Contrast	instead, however, by contrast
Emphasis	indeed, in fact, undoubtedly

Work It Out

A *Complete the sentences with **however** and correct punctuation.*

① Jean wanted to play tennis. _____ she couldn't find anyone to play with.

② I know you don't like vegetables _____ you should eat some every day because they're good for you.

③ He studied hard. His score _____ wasn't very good.

B *Fill in the blanks with the words in the box.*

> therefore / indeed / instead / furthermore / by contrast

① Helen was sick. _____, she didn't go to the party.

② I was going to go to Jack's party, but I stayed home _____.

③ Anna loves to meet new friends. _____, her sister Elsa prefers to be alone.

④ That movie is hilarious. The actors are very funny _____.

⑤ This apartment is beautiful and centrally located. _____, the rent is not very high.

Yesterday's Technology Makes a Comeback

CD 2-04

With constant advances in today's technology, the latest models of modern gadgets are always in demand. It may therefore come as a surprise that there has been a recent increase in the popularity of certain older technologies. For those who
5　miss these older products—or simply want something different—there is no replacement for their unique appeal. Cell phones are constantly being improved with things like more advanced cameras, faster network connections, and sharper screens. However, sales of old and used cell phones that can do little more than text and call have recently begun to rise dramatically. Mobile phone producer
10　Nokia is even releasing a new version of its classic Nokia 3310.

The music world has also seen increased interest in old technologies. In fact, in December 2016, vinyl record sales actually overtook digital music sales in the United Kingdom for the first time ever. Music lovers explain this shift by pointing to the distinct, warm sound that only vinyl can provide. Others say they enjoy
15　holding onto the physical record or listening to certain older albums in the format they were originally made for. Much like for vinyl, sales of cassette tapes have also risen lately. As technology continues to advance, these recent trends remind us that the newest product isn't necessarily the best for everyone. It just goes to show that regardless of age, the real value of a thing is the value we give it personally.

A *Fill in the blanks with the word choices given. Change the word form if necessary.*

advanced / regardless / gadget / overtake / dramatically

1. Your life changes _____ when you have a baby to take care of.

2. Please call me when you get home, _____ of the time.

3. This dance class will teach you some _____ moves that are more difficult to do.

4. This _____ is for peeling avocados.

5. Our U.S. sales have now _____ our sales in Europe.

B *Check the correct answers.*

1. What's the article mainly about?
   - ☐ **a.** The latest technology of cell phones
   - ☐ **b.** The reasons why old technology has gotten popular again
   - ☐ **c.** The recent trends in home appliances

2. Which is NOT mentioned about the improvement of cell phones?
   - ☐ **a.** Endless battery life
   - ☐ **b.** Faster network connections
   - ☐ **c.** Sharper screens

3. What do we know about Nokia?
   - ☐ **a.** It specializes in making classical music.
   - ☐ **b.** It produced a cell phone called the 3310.
   - ☐ **c.** It has only produced cell phones.

4. What does the article suggest?
   - ☐ **a.** Yesterday's technology will replace the newest technology.
   - ☐ **b.** We cannot keep up with technology.
   - ☐ **c.** The advanced product isn't the best for everyone.

5. Which of the following statements is correct?
   - ☐ **a.** Cassette tapes sold more than digital music in 2016 in the United Kingdom.
   - ☐ **b.** Vinyl records sold more than digital music in December 2016 in the United Kingdom.
   - ☐ **c.** Sales of cassette tapes showed a sharp decrease recently.

Do you know any other old technologies? What are their features? List and discuss them with your class.

Product Name:	Features:
Floppy Disk	They come in several sizes.

WRITING

Here are two amazing inventions that can make life easier. Read the sample article and create your own invention. Write 80-100 words about your invention.

Pet Translator

Are you curious about what your pets are thinking? Are they hungry? Do they like their food? Are they ill? Then this is the invention for YOU! Now, with this whistle, you can easily understand your pets' needs. Pet Whistle comes in four languages—English, Chinese, Japanese, and French.

Memory Donuts

Do you always forget something really important? Is your teacher mad because you forgot to hand in your report? Do your friends ignore you because you forget about bowling night? Eat memory donuts, and you won't forget about anything again. Choose from many flavors—strawberry, chocolate, mango, vanilla, taro, coffee, and peanut.

More good news If you buy 10 dozen memory donuts, you get weight loss classes for FREE.

CHALLENGE YOURSELF

Part I Pictures 🎧 2-05

Look at the picture and choose the best answer.

1.

Cut it into small pieces.

☐ a   ☐ b   ☐ c

2.

☐ a   ☐ b   ☐ c

Part II Question & Response 🎧 2-06

Listen to the statement or question and choose the best response.

3. ☐ a   ☐ b   ☐ c   5. ☐ a   ☐ b   ☐ c
4. ☐ a   ☐ b   ☐ c   6. ☐ a   ☐ b   ☐ c

Part III Conversations 🎧 2-07

Listen to the conversation and answer the questions.

7. What doesn't the man like?
   ☐ a. The kitchen and bathrooms
   ☐ b. The tables and chairs
   ☐ c. The color of the walls

8. What does the woman want to buy?
   ☐ a. Something that heats up food
   ☐ b. Something that stores food
   ☐ c. Something that makes food cold

9. Where is the conversation probably taking place?
   ☐ a. In a library
   ☐ b. In an electronics store
   ☐ c. In a convenience store

10. What does the man want to do?
   ☐ a. Clean the kitchen
   ☐ b. Replace the cabinets
   ☐ c. Hire a personal chef

Linguaporta Training

Let's review the unit with Linguaporta.

UNIT 07

TECHNOLOGY IN DAILY LIFE

83

WARM UP

TALK ABOUT THIS

Talk about these questions.

Have you ever made a friend on the Internet?

ACTIVATE

Ⓐ *Listen to the conversations and choose the correct pictures.* 🎧 2-08

Question 1.	Question 2.

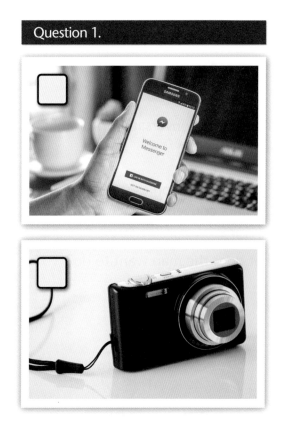

Do you prefer cute stickers or funny stickers? And do you spend money on app stickers?

B *Role-play with a partner. Extend the conversation as much as you can.*

Ⓐ Do you like _____ stickers?

Ⓑ • Yeah, I love them!

• No, I hate them.

....

Ⓐ What do you do on that app?

Ⓑ Oh, I like to _____ .

....

Ⓐ How many times do you check _____ every day?

Ⓑ _____ .

Question 3.

Meeting an Online Friend

A *Watch the video clip and check the correct answers.*

1. What kind of group does Ellen belong to?
   - ☐ **a.** A photography group
   - ☐ **b.** A computer science group
   - ☐ **c.** A painting group

2. How long has Ellen known her online friends?
   - ☐ **a.** For weeks
   - ☐ **b.** For months
   - ☐ **c.** For years

3. Where will Ellen meet her group?
   - ☐ **a.** At a department store
   - ☐ **b.** At a coffee shop
   - ☐ **c.** At a public park

4. What does Ron have to do before going with Ellen?
   - ☐ **a.** Send an e-mail
   - ☐ **b.** Tell someone where he's going
   - ☐ **c.** Shower and change

B *Listen to the conversation and fill in the blanks.* 🎧 2-09 💻WEB動画

Ron is exercising in the living room, where his sister Ellen is laughing at something she is reading on her laptop.

Ron: What are you laughing at?

Ellen: Oh, SmartShot18 just made a joke. He's the funniest member of our ¹_____ group.

Ron: Are you even sure he's a guy? You can't really tell anything about so-called friends online. They could be anyone.

Ellen: Well, I guess I'll find out. A few of us are meeting up this afternoon.

Ron: What?! Ellen, that could be ²_____ dangerous! You can't go!

Ellen: Don't be so worried, Ron. I've been chatting with these people for ³_____. They're all ⁴_____ people who are interested in photography.

Ron: They could be nice people, but you should still take some ⁵_____ to make sure you're safe.

Ellen: What do you suggest?

Ron: The first meeting should always be in a busy ⁶_____ place.

Ellen: We're meeting at a coffee shop, so that's not a problem.

Ron: Second, tell someone where you are going, how long you'll be there, and information about the people you are meeting.

Ellen: I'll write that down and give it to you.

Ron: Actually, you really should bring someone you trust with you. That would be the ⁷_____ action.

Ellen: Oh. I don't know anyone I can ask.

Ron: Well, give me a few minutes to ⁸_____ and change, and I'll be happy to go with you.

C *Practice the conversation with your partner.*

D *Listen to the conversation and check what the man looks like.* 🎧 2-10

GRAMMAR　　Noun Clauses

A noun clause is a dependent clause that functions as a noun. It can be a subject, an object, or a complement.

That Clauses

- <u>That she was late again</u> is not surprising.

  S.

  = It is not surprising <u>that she was late again</u>.

  ↳ *as a subject*

- Jason believes <u>(that) smoking is a terrible habit</u>.

  ↳ *as an object of a verb*

- The truth is <u>that the rich get richer and the poor get poorer</u>.

  ↳ *as a complement*

Wh-words

- <u>What he said</u> is not true.

  ↳ *as a subject*

- I wonder <u>when Frank will come</u>.

  ↳ *as an object of a verb*

- The problem is <u>who would want to do this difficult job</u>.

  ↳ *as a complement*

- The fact is <u>what you do doesn't matter</u>.

- The point is <u>how you deal with your boss</u>.

Whether, If

*To change a yes/no question to a noun clause, use **if** or **whether**.*

- <u>Whether we will go</u> depends on the weather.

  ↳ *as a subject*

- I don't know <u>whether/if we can keep the dog</u>.

  ↳ *as an object of a verb*

- Bob asked <u>whether he could have the last cookie or not</u>.

- Sarah wonders <u>whether/if she will pass the exam</u>.

- We should decide <u>whether/if we need a new editor</u>.

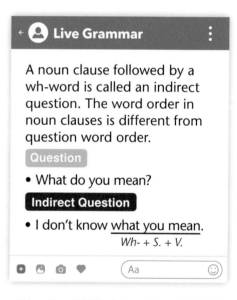

← 👤 **Live Grammar** ⋮

A noun clause followed by a wh-word is called an indirect question. The word order in noun clauses is different from question word order.

`Question`

- What do you mean?

`Indirect Question`

- I don't know <u>what you mean</u>.

  Wh- + S. + V.

➕ 🖼 📷 ♥　(Aa 　☺)

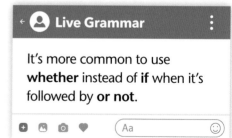

← 👤 **Live Grammar** ⋮

It's more common to use **whether** instead of **if** when it's followed by **or not**.

➕ 🖼 📷 ♥　(Aa 　☺)

Work It Out

Ⓐ *Fill in the blanks with **that** or a **wh-word**.*

① The trouble is _____ she is late almost every day.

② Sarah thinks that _____ Andy believes is wrong.

③ Don finally admitted _____ he cheated on the test.

④ It is still a secret _____ Mr. Black married Jean last month.

Ⓑ *Combine the two sentences based on the hints given.*

① { I'm not sure.
  { Did Lisa wash the clothes? (whether)

_____

② { Mark can't remember.
  { Did he see that movie? (if)

_____

③ { Does Paula like him?
  { Henry is wondering. (whether ... or not)

_____

④ { Who was that very tall man at the door?
  { No one knows. (who)

_____

⑤ { That is the most important thing.
  { How will they get to the train station? (how)

_____

⑥ { I don't want to fight about that.
  { We should buy a new TV. (whether ... or not)

_____

App Stickers' Popularity

2-11

The craze for app stickers is taking over Asia, with Cony, Brown, Hello Kitty, and other characters gracing billions of mobile app messages each day. These digital stickers are also responsible for the popularity of Asian app giants like LINE, WeChat, and KakaoTalk. Stickers are popular in Asia because they can be used as a sort of
5   visual shorthand. Typing Asian characters using smartphones designed with the Latin alphabet may be tiring. Also, with stickers, users can also express ideas indirectly, thus avoiding embarrassment or offending people.

Now, these services are looking to enter North America. But what kind of stickers become popular will depend on the market. To begin with, the cute stickers that are
10   popular in Asia may be considered childish by North Americans. Also, many English speakers may not find writing text messages time-consuming. In fact, many common expressions are typed using abbreviations, such as TTYL for "talk to you later" and BTW for "by the way." North Americans also tend to be verbally direct, which means they don't need to use stickers as a subtle form of communication. To be profitable in
15   North America, where the no-sticker WhatsApp is currently the preferred messaging app, it's up to companies like LINE to make stickers that will actually stick. Whether that will happen remains to be seen.

A *Fill in the blanks with the word choices given. Change the word form if necessary.*

craze / embarrassment / profitable / tend / subtle

1. The company had to cut 300 jobs to stay _____.

2. The _____ for health foods has become big business.

3. They say it _____ to rain a lot this time of the year.

4. There is a(n) _____ difference between these two plans.

5. To her _____, she couldn't remember his name.

B *Check the correct answers.*

1. Why are stickers popular in Asia?
   - ☐ a. They can replace words.
   - ☐ b. They are always free.
   - ☐ c. They are quite tiring.

2. What can users do with stickers?
   - ☐ a. Speak directly
   - ☐ b. Type Latin letters of the alphabet
   - ☐ c. Express ideas without embarrassing people

3. What may North Americans think about cute stickers?
   - ☐ a. They are for children.
   - ☐ b. They take too much time.
   - ☐ c. They are best for adults.

4. According to the article, which is NOT an abbreviation used by North Americans?
   - ☐ a. BTW
   - ☐ b. TTYL
   - ☐ c. WTWB

5. According to the article, which messaging app is most popular in North America?
   - ☐ a. LINE
   - ☐ b. WeChat
   - ☐ c. WhatsApp

Look at the pictures. What do the following stickers likely mean?

I AM SO MAD. _____ _____ _____ _____

WRITING

What did you do today? How do you feel? Read the sample and update your status on social network sites.

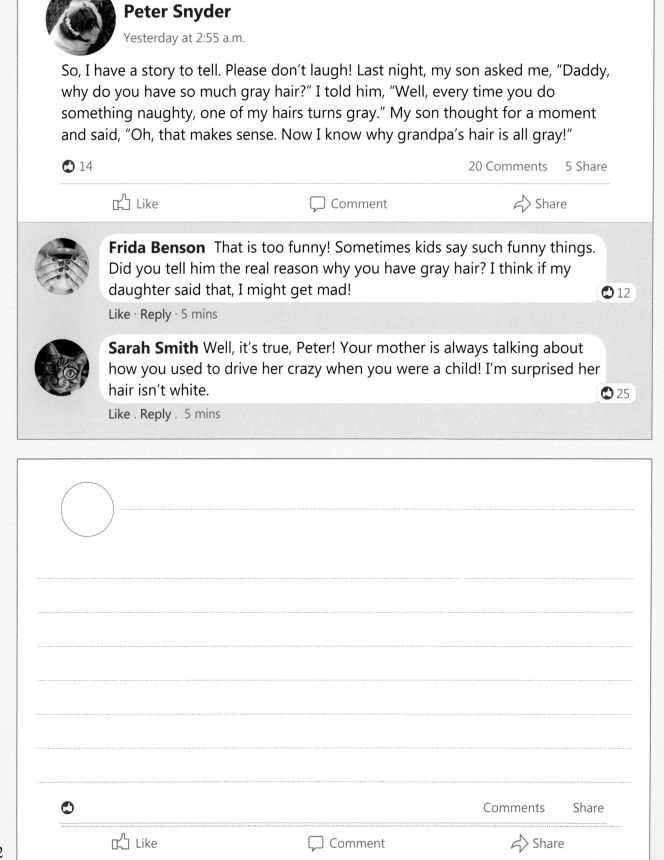

Peter Snyder
Yesterday at 2:55 a.m.

So, I have a story to tell. Please don't laugh! Last night, my son asked me, "Daddy, why do you have so much gray hair?" I told him, "Well, every time you do something naughty, one of my hairs turns gray." My son thought for a moment and said, "Oh, that makes sense. Now I know why grandpa's hair is all gray!"

👍 14   20 Comments   5 Share

👍 Like   💬 Comment   ➦ Share

Frida Benson That is too funny! Sometimes kids say such funny things. Did you tell him the real reason why you have gray hair? I think if my daughter said that, I might get mad!   👍 12

Like · Reply · 5 mins

Sarah Smith Well, it's true, Peter! Your mother is always talking about how you used to drive her crazy when you were a child! I'm surprised her hair isn't white.   👍 25

Like . Reply . 5 mins

👍   Comments   Share

👍 Like   💬 Comment   ➦ Share

CHALLENGE YOURSELF

Part I Pictures 🎧 2-12

Look at the picture and choose the best answer.

1.

☐ a   ☐ b   ☐ c

2.

☐ a   ☐ b   ☐ c

Part II Question & Response 🎧 2-13

Listen to the statement or question and choose the best response.

3. ☐ a   ☐ b   ☐ c   **5.** ☐ a   ☐ b   ☐ c
4. ☐ a   ☐ b   ☐ c   **6.** ☐ a   ☐ b   ☐ c

Part III Conversations 🎧 2-14

Listen to the conversation and answer the questions.

7. What is the woman going to do?
☐ a. Take more pictures
☐ b. Give the camera to the man
☐ c. Put the pictures online

8. What does the man say about his work?
☐ a. It's regular.
☐ b. It's hard.
☐ c. It's fun.

9. What does the woman mean?
☐ a. She knows Gabe is full.
☐ b. She thinks Gabe should eat.
☐ c. She will make food for Gabe.

10. What does the woman say?
☐ a. She would like to find more schools.
☐ b. She wants the man to decide for her.
☐ c. She wants to know more about the schools.

Linguaporta Training

Let's review the unit with Linguaporta.

Looking on the Bright Side

TALK ABOUT THIS

Talk about these questions.

Why is it good to stay positive?

ACTIVATE

A *Listen and look at the pictures below. What do you think is happening in each picture?* 🎧 2-15

What do positive thoughts do to your brain?

B *Listen to the introduction again and number the sentences in order. Write the numbers in the box below.*

| 1 | Over the course of our lives, there are many things that might bring us down. |

Staying positive is important for our mental and physical health. When we let negative thoughts remain in our minds, they can cause stress or affect our sleep.

Life is too short to let sad, frustrating, or hurtful things get us down. Exercise, talk to someone, eat something nice—don't dwell on the negatives.

With a little positivity, you will become a better and happier person.

To prevent this, the best thing to do is to look at situations from a positive angle. If that's too hard, find someone who can help you look for positives.

You might get a bad grade, get in a fight with your friend, or even have trouble at home. But no matter what happens, remember to try and stay positive.

Staying Positive

Ⓐ *Watch the video clip and check the correct answers.*

1. What does Theresa mean when she says that Vince looks "down in the dumps"?
   ☐ **a.** He looks poor and dirty.
   ☐ **b.** He looks tired.
   ☐ **c.** He seems depressed.

2. What advice does Theresa give to Vince regarding his painting?
   ☐ **a.** To try and ignore criticism
   ☐ **b.** To show his work to some art collectors
   ☐ **c.** To focus more on getting others' approval

3. What will Vince likely do?
   ☐ **a.** Give up painting
   ☐ **b.** Continue sharing his paintings
   ☐ **c.** Never show anyone his paintings

4. Why does Vince feel better?
   ☐ **a.** Because he read a positive comment on Facebook.
   ☐ **b.** Because he took some time to think about things.
   ☐ **c.** Because his friend encouraged him.

B *Listen to the conversation and fill in the blanks.* 🎧 2-16 📺

Vince and Theresa are sitting on a park bench.

Theresa: Is something wrong, Vince? You look down in the dumps.

Vince: Yeah, something is ¹_____ me. But I don't feel like talking about it.

Theresa: Come on. Sometimes it helps to share your problems with another person.

Vince: All right. I ²_____ a picture of one of my paintings on Facebook.

Theresa: You mean the one of the village? I saw that. It's great!

Vince: I guess you're the only one, then. Some people wrote some comments about it that weren't very ³_____.

Theresa: No way! What did they say?

Vince: One said it looked like my little brother had painted it. My brother is four, by the way. Then, another said it ⁴_____ a monkey's work.

Theresa: Oh, Vince. I'm so sorry this happened to you. But you've got to keep your ⁵_____ up. Don't pay any attention to those ⁶_____.

Vince: Why? What if they have a point?

Theresa: Because life is about doing what you believe in. It's not about ⁷_____ thumbs-ups.

Vince: So, do you think I should keep sharing pictures of my paintings?

Theresa: Most certainly. A true artist must put himself or herself out there. Ignore criticism.

Vince: Thanks for the ⁸_____. I felt bad before, but now I'm much better.

C *Practice the conversation with your partner.*

D *Match the pictures with the correct expressions.*

    thumbs-up   **down in the dumps**   **keep one's chin up**

*A **linking verb** connects a subject to its complement.*

> S. + **be** + { **adj.**
> { **N.**

• Your sister **is** <u>very cute</u>.
↳ *adjective as a complement*

• Tom's brother **is** <u>a basketball player</u>.
↳ *noun as a complement*

> S. + **Sense Verbs** + { **adj.**
> { **like + N.**

• Your grandfather **looks** old but happy.

• The coffee **smells** wonderful.

• Kevin's eyes **look** like his father's.

• The new movie **sounds** exciting!

> S. + { **get**
> { **keep** } + { **adj.**
> { **become** } { **N.**

• It's **getting** dark.

• My parents are **growing** old.

• The baby **kept** quiet all night long.

• I **became** a writer after I finished university.

Live Grammar

Here is the way to tell whether a verb is an action verb or a linking verb.

• Laura <u>looked</u> tired.
↳ *it can be replaced with **is**, so it is a linking verb*

• Laura <u>looked</u> at me carefully.
↳ *it CANNOT be replaced with **is**, so it's an action verb*

Aa

Work It Out

A *Check the correct answers.*

① My head feels (☐ heavy / ☐ heavily).

② The coffee tastes (☐ like / ☐ ×) medicine.

③ Elaine (☐ looks / ☐ looks like) her mother, so she (☐ looks / ☐ looks like) beautiful.

④ It's getting (☐ dark / ☐ darkly). It's time to go home.

⑤ John appeared (☐ happily / ☐ happy) when the company promoted him.

GRAMMAR 2 –ing adjectives VS. –ed adjectives

*Both **-ing adjectives** and **-ed adjectives** are formed from the base forms of verbs. Present participles (-ing) are used to describe something or someone. Past participles (-ed) are used to describe how people feel about something or someone.*

The soccer game is **exciting**.

The boys are **excited**.

```
S. + be + V-ing + (to sb)
S. + be + V-ed + prep.
```

- The soccer game **excited** the boys.
  V.

- The soccer game is **exciting** to the boys.
  V-ing

- The boys **are excited about** the soccer game.
  be + V-ed + prep.

Live Grammar

- be interested in
- be surprised at/by
- be tired of
- be excited at/about
- be bored with
- be satisfied with

(Aa)

Work It Out

Ⓐ *Fill in the blanks based on the hints given.*

① If you are _____, why don't you clean your room? (bore)

② Charles felt very _____ at the news. (surprise)

③ If you're willing to try new things, you will have an _____ life. (excite)

④ The movie was _____, so I went to sleep. (bore)

⑤ I was _____ and went to bed early. (tire)

Ⓑ *Look at the pictures and write sentences based on the hints given.*

① The pile of work bored the woman.

The pile of work was boring to the woman.
(V-ing)

_____
(V-ed)

② The novel interested Tracy.

_____
(V-ing)

_____
(V-ed)

③ The news surprised David.

_____
(V-ing)

_____
(V-ed)

UNIT
09

LOOKING ON THE BRIGHT SIDE

99

2-17

I used to work at a shop with a man named Jake. He always had a smile on his face. Even when things went wrong, he never got upset. He saw the positive side to any problem. He always said, "Come on, try to look on the bright side."

One day, our boss said he wanted to talk to us. The boss looked super serious.
5   I was really worried, but Jake looked totally fine! So we went into our boss's office. He said he was going to shut down the shop. We would lose our jobs in a month. I was shocked. I wanted to cry! Then I looked at Jake. He looked happy! "We have a whole month," he said. "That's lots of time to find new jobs!"

It surprised me that Jake could still be so positive. After all, we just got terrible
10 news. I asked him why he wasn't upset. Jake said that life was about choices. You can choose to be upset, or you can choose to think positively. If you choose to think positively, bad things won't look bad. They will look like opportunities.

Jake and I both have different jobs now. However, I never forgot what
15 he said. Now, when I face difficulties, I choose to think positively. I'm confident that I'm making a good choice.

A *Fill in the blanks with the word choices given. Change the word form if necessary.*

> upset / confident / whole / totally / opportunity

1. I read the _____ book in one day.

2. We used to go out dancing, but we don't have much _____ now.

3. We're _____ next year's profits will be higher.

4. My boyfriend was _____ because I forgot his birthday.

5. His second wife is _____ different from his first one.

B *Check the correct answers.*

1. What's the main idea of the article?
   - ☐ **a.** How to talk to your boss
   - ☐ **b.** How to stay positive
   - ☐ **c.** How to find a new job

2. Who is Jake?
   - ☐ **a.** The writer's brother
   - ☐ **b.** The writer's colleague
   - ☐ **c.** The writer's boss

3. What was the boss going to do?
   - ☐ **a.** Close his store
   - ☐ **b.** Give the writer a new job
   - ☐ **c.** Give the writer a month of vacation

4. How did the writer feel when he got the bad news?
   - ☐ **a.** Sad
   - ☐ **b.** Excited
   - ☐ **c.** Happy

5. Why did Jake look happy when he got the terrible news?
   - ☐ **a.** He thought he had no choice.
   - ☐ **b.** He wanted to quit the job.
   - ☐ **c.** He chose to look on the bright side.

Here are some quotes about positive thinking. Which do you like? Why?

"I've had a lot of worries in my life, most of which never happened." – Mark Twain

"The past has no power over the present moment." – Eckhart Tolle

"Hope is a waking dream." – Aristotle

WRITING

Read the following passage. It describes ways to get happier. Try to list some of your own.

Are you happy? Modern people are often too stressed out by their schoolwork or their jobs. Sometimes they forget how to be happy. The following are some suggestions that would make you feel happier.

1. Laugh out loud.
It doesn't matter if you smile, grin, giggle, or laugh like crazy. You'll be happy as long as you laugh out loud.

2. Get enough sleep.
Getting enough sleep is the key to a healthy life. Once you start to sleep well, you'll be happy!

3. Make time for your dream.
Our dreams make us great. If you have a dream and you work toward it every day, you'll achieve it someday.

4. Stop complaining.
Have you ever noticed that when people are complaining, they are usually frowning, too? If you stop complaining, your face will look much better.

5. Travel.
The good thing about traveling is that you can leave your troubles at home. When you're busy having fun, you won't have enough time to be unhappy.

CHALLENGE YOURSELF

Part I Pictures 🔊 2-18

Look at the picture and choose the best answer.

1.

☐ a   ☐ b   ☐ c

2.

☐ a   ☐ b   ☐ c

Part II Question & Response 🔊 2-19

Listen to the statement or question and choose the best response.

3. ☐ a   ☐ b   ☐ c   5. ☐ a   ☐ b   ☐ c
4. ☐ a   ☐ b   ☐ c   6. ☐ a   ☐ b   ☐ c

Part III Conversations 🔊 2-20

Listen to the conversation and answer the questions.

7. What is the man telling the woman to do?
   ☐ a. Think in a good way
   ☐ b. Give up on finding a job
   ☐ c. Take a month off

8. What do we know about Dan?
   ☐ a. He's sad now.
   ☐ b. He tends to think positively.
   ☐ c. He's surprised to hear about the bad news.

9. What does the man mean?
   ☐ a. He has a favor to ask the woman.
   ☐ b. He feels bad for asking the woman's help.
   ☐ c. He's thanking the woman for her help.

10. How does Bobby feel about his math score?
   ☐ a. He's happy about it.
   ☐ b. He's sad about it.
   ☐ c. He doesn't say.

Linguaporta Training

Let's review the unit with Linguaporta.

UNIT 10

Love Affairs

TALK ABOUT THIS

Talk about these questions.

> What kind of relationship do you think is the best?

ACTIVATE

A *Listen to the conversations and choose the correct pictures.* 🔵 **CD** 2-21

Question 1.

Question 2.

Do you believe in love at first sight?

Question 3.

B *Role-play with a partner. Extend the conversation as much as you can.*

Ⓐ Happy Valentine's Day!

Ⓑ Wow, thank you! These _____ are so _____.

....

Ⓐ Who's the guy / girl in the picture with you?

Ⓑ His / Her name's _____.

Keeping It Casual?

A *Watch the video clip and check the correct answers.* WEB動画 🖥️

1. What's Daniel and Karen's relationship?
   - ☐ **a.** They were lovers.
   - ☐ **b.** They were roommates.
   - ☐ **c.** They were classmates.

2. Where are Mari and Michelino from?
   - ☐ **a.** France and London
   - ☐ **b.** India and Italy
   - ☐ **c.** None of the above

3. Who does NOT approve of a foreign affair?
   - ☐ **a.** Karen
   - ☐ **b.** Daniel
   - ☐ **c.** Both of them

4. According to Karen, what should Mari and Michelino do?
   - ☐ **a.** Get married as soon as possible
   - ☐ **b.** Break up as soon as possible
   - ☐ **c.** Just continue to date each other

B *Listen to the conversation and fill in the blanks.* 🎧 2-22 📺

Karen is logging into Skype.

Daniel: Hello!

Karen: Who are you? Do I know you?

Daniel: Sorry. I don't mean to ¹_____ you. I just happened to see your ID and thought you were a classmate from the language school I ²_____ years ago.

Karen: Frances King London? Are you Daniel Jones?

Daniel: That's me!

Karen: Wow, I can't believe it!

Daniel: It's really amazing to ³_____ with you again. By the way, have you read Mari and Michelino's story on LINE?

Karen: Yeah, I did. Personally, I think it's going to be a sad ending to a foreign affair.

Daniel: What ⁴_____ you think so?

Karen: I just can't imagine how difficult it would be to keep a ⁵_____ cultural love affair alive.

Daniel: ⁶_____ the power of love overcome all obstacles?

Karen: Well, love is great, but there are always other ⁷_____ lovebirds need to consider.

Daniel: So you mean that simply dating would be much better for them?

Karen: Yeah, life is short. Why bother getting yourself into a ⁸_____ when you can sense trouble right from the very beginning?

Daniel: OK, I see. I don't know. Maybe I should name you the "Risk Sensor."

Karen: Call me the "Freedom Lover!"

C *Practice the conversation with your partner.*

D *Discuss the following with your classmates.*

- Can a long-distance relationship work?
- Do you think love can overcome anything?

A relative pronoun is used to refer to nouns mentioned previously. They can be used to join two sentences.

	Person	Thing/Animal
Subject	who, that	which, that
Object	who, whom, that	which, that
Possessive	whose	whose

As a subject

• **The man** lives next door. / **He** is very handsome.
    subject   *subject*

        The man **who** lives next door is very handsome.
  antecedent   ↳*relative pronoun referring to a person*

    = The man **that** lives next door is very handsome.
  antecedent   ↳*relative pronoun*

• **The red car** hit the mailbox and it drove off.
    subject

        The red car **which** hit the mailbox drove off.
  antecedent   ↳*relative pronoun referring to a thing or an animal*

    = The red car **that** hit the mailbox drove off.
  antecedent   ↳*relative pronoun*

As an object

• I met a **funny girl** yesterday. / The **funny girl** was your sister.
        object   *subject*

        The funny girl **whom** I met yesterday was your sister.
  antecedent   ↳*relative pronoun referring to a person*

    = The funny girl **that** I met yesterday was your sister.
  antecedent   ↳*relative pronoun*

• I've found the **car keys**. / You were looking for **them**.
        object   *object*

    I've found the car keys **which** you were looking for.
    antecedent   ↳*relative pronoun referring to a thing or an animal*

    = I've found the car keys **that** you were looking for.
    antecedent   ↳*relative pronoun*

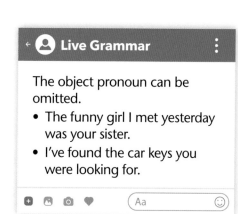

← 👤 **Live Grammar** ⋮

The object pronoun can be omitted.
• The funny girl I met yesterday was your sister.
• I've found the car keys you were looking for.

➕ 🖼 📷 ♥   (Aa   ☺)

108

As possessive

- **The boy's** mother left, and he was crying.
  possessive

  ↓

  The boy **whose** mother left was crying.
  antecedent ↵   ↳*relative pronoun referring to a person (or thing)*

Whose + noun can be the subject or object

- The stereo **whose case** is purple belongs to Adam.
  subject
- The student **whose picture** I just took will graduate next year.
  object

← 👤 **Live Grammar** ⋮

In some cases, we use *that* instead of *which*.
1. After the nouns **all, any, every, few, little, no**.
2. After a noun modified by a superlative adjective.
- This is the best movie that I've ever seen.

➕ 🖼 📷 ❤   (Aa)   ☺

Work It Out

A *Check the correct answers.*

① He's a person (☐ which / ☐ who) likes to listen to music when he works.

② Jane and Sally are the ones (☐ that / ☐ which) can't come to the party.

③ The pizza (☐ who / ☐ which) tastes good comes from Pizza House.

④ What was the name of the boy (☐ who / ☐ which) said hello to you?

B *Check the correct answers.*

Dear Diary,

  I've been in love with a boy for one year. The boy, (☐ who / ☐ whose) name is Ted, is my classmate. Today, I saw the boy (☐ which / ☐ whom) I love holding a girl's hand. My friend told me she's the one (☐ who / ☐ whom) is the boy's new girlfriend. I'm so upset, because he's the first boy (☐ which / ☐ that) I really want to be with. What should I do?

Sad,
Me

C *Combine the two sentences based on the hints given.*

① { I have a brother.
  { He works for a high-tech company. (who)

  _____

② { I can trust Jim.
  { I can't trust other people. (that)

  Jim is the only person _____

③ { I have a friend.
  { His father is a popular actor. (whose)

  _____

Arranged Marriage

2-23

To most of us, marrying someone we are madly in love with is something we look forward to. But for people in some cultures, love has nothing to do with marriage. They have to wed whomever their parents decide is best for them. Sometimes they wed for their family's sake.

5　　In India, for instance, it's common for parents to look for a bride or groom for their child and for the couple to be married within weeks of meeting. To say "no" is to disrespect the wishes of the family, so many people end up marrying someone that they hardly know, let alone love.

Supporters believe there is much to be said for arranged marriage. They say
10　that love can blind a person's logic—having one's family choose one's <u>spouse</u> is a safer way to ensure a successful marriage. They also point out the low rate of divorce among arranged marriages.

Those against arranged marriage say that forcing people to wed someone they haven't chosen themselves is against human rights. They believe that the
15　lower divorce rate is due to family and social pressure and not because of happier or more successful marriages.

Happily, though, some arranged couples do end up falling in love—but could that really be called a marriage made in heaven?

A *Fill in the blanks with the word choices given. Change the word form if necessary.*

> sake / disrespect / logic / instance / married

1. We need to get more exercise. For _____, we could go jogging.

2. Don't _____ what I believe in.

3. Chris and Danielle are getting _____ next month.

4. I can't see the _____ behind his argument.

5. Their parents only stayed together for the _____ of the children.

B *Check the correct answers.*

1. What is the main idea of the article?
   - ☐ **a.** To explain the good and bad points of arranged marriages
   - ☐ **b.** To show that arranged marriages are often very successful
   - ☐ **c.** To tell people more about marriage customs in India

2. According to the article, what is something good most of us enjoy waiting for?
   - ☐ **a.** Marrying someone who is crazy
   - ☐ **b.** Marrying someone who loves something
   - ☐ **c.** Marrying someone we really love

3. What does the underlined word "spouse" mean?
   - ☐ **a.** Husband or wife
   - ☐ **b.** Child
   - ☐ **c.** Destiny

4. What do supporters of arranged marriage believe?
   - ☐ **a.** That it needs to be discussed a lot
   - ☐ **b.** That there are good things about it
   - ☐ **c.** That people talk too much about it

5. According to supporters of arranged marriage, what can love do to a person?
   - ☐ **a.** Make them very sad
   - ☐ **b.** Make them think unclearly
   - ☐ **c.** Make them want to fly away

Write down the features of your perfect match.

ex.) <u>Has good taste in music, or at least similar taste in music to mine.</u>

1. _____

2. _____

3. _____

WRITING

This is your chance! Write a text message to that special person you want to go out with. Using the message below as a model, write your information. Write 60-70 words.

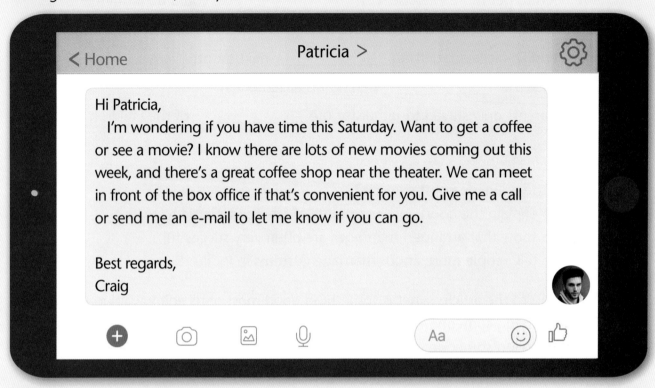

Patricia >

< Home

Hi Patricia,

I'm wondering if you have time this Saturday. Want to get a coffee or see a movie? I know there are lots of new movies coming out this week, and there's a great coffee shop near the theater. We can meet in front of the box office if that's convenient for you. Give me a call or send me an e-mail to let me know if you can go.

Best regards,
Craig

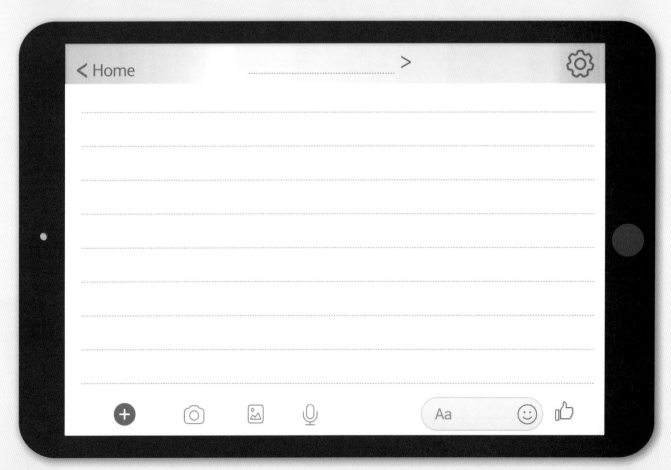

< Home

CHALLENGE YOURSELF

Part I Pictures 🔊 2-24

Look at the picture and choose the best answer.

1.

☐ a ☐ b ☐ c

2.

☐ a ☐ b ☐ c

Part II Question & Response 🔊 2-25

Listen to the statement or question and choose the best response.

3. ☐ a ☐ b ☐ c   5. ☐ a ☐ b ☐ c
4. ☐ a ☐ b ☐ c   6. ☐ a ☐ b ☐ c

Part III Conversations 🔊 2-26

Listen to the conversation and answer the questions.

7. What does the man say about England?
   ☐ a. It's much cheaper to buy the tickets there.
   ☐ b. Many people there go traveling before going to university.
   ☐ c. He'll spend a lot of his time traveling there.

8. What is the woman telling the man?
   ☐ a. She thinks that he did the right thing.
   ☐ b. She thinks he accidentally said something.
   ☐ c. She thinks he disrespected his grandmother.

9. What is the woman doing to the man?
   ☐ a. She's having a love affair with him.
   ☐ b. She's bothering him.
   ☐ c. She's sensing trouble.

10. What do we know about Ray and his girlfriend?
   ☐ a. They're really in love.
   ☐ b. They met last weekend.
   ☐ c. They're not dating anymore.

Linguaporta Training

Let's review the unit with Linguaporta.

UNIT
10

LOVE AFFAIRS

113

UNIT 11

Storytelling

TALK ABOUT THIS

Talk about these questions.

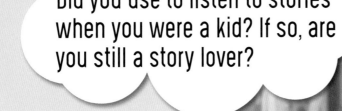

Did you use to listen to stories when you were a kid? If so, are you still a story lover?

ACTIVATE

A *Listen and look at the pictures below. What do you think is happening in each picture?* 2-27

The Wind and the Sun

The Boy Who Cried Wolf

The Thirsty Crow

The City Mouse and the Country Mouse

What fables have you heard before?

The King and His Two Wives

The Tortoise and the Hare

B *Listen to the introduction again and number the sentences in order. Write the numbers in the boxes below.*

☐ The lesson is usually told at the end of the story.

☐ Animals are often the main characters in fables, but they speak and act just like humans.

1 A fable is a short story that not only entertains, but also tries to teach the reader a moral lesson.

☐ Most important is that he used humble stories to teach others great truths and right from wrong.

☐ Aesop's fables have reached countless generations since he lived, and they continue to be a part of our lives.

☐ The most famous author of fables was a man called Aesop, who lived in Greece in the sixth century B.C.

Honesty Is the Best Policy

A *Watch the video clip and check the correct answers.* WEB動画 🖥️📱

1. How does Karen know Danny didn't do his assignment himself?
   - ☐ **a.** From the excuse that he gives her
   - ☐ **b.** From the look that he has on his face
   - ☐ **c.** From the handwriting on his assignment

2. What's the point of the fable?
   - ☐ **a.** Honesty is the best policy.
   - ☐ **b.** Better late than never.
   - ☐ **c.** The early bird gets the worm.

3. Why did the fairy give a new golden ax to the woodsman?
   - ☐ **a.** Because the woodsman had told her the truth.
   - ☐ **b.** Because she didn't have an old ax to give him.
   - ☐ **c.** Because she was touched by the story.

4. Which statement is true?
   - ☐ **a.** The little fairy gave the woodsman an old ax.
   - ☐ **b.** The woodsman lived next to a stream.
   - ☐ **c.** The woodsman lost an iron ax.

B *Listen to the conversation and fill in the blanks.* 🎧 2-28 🖥️

Karen works as an assistant at a cram school. Danny is a junior high student.

Karen: Danny, did you hand in your assignment yesterday?

Danny: No, but I have it now.

Karen: Why didn't you turn it in yesterday?

Danny: I [1]_____ forgot.

Karen: Wait! The handwriting looks different! Did you do it yourself?

Danny: Of course! I [2]_____ up late finishing it last night.

Karen: Sorry, but I don't think it's your handwriting, Danny. I'm getting angry now. You better tell me the truth!

Danny: Sorry, Karen. My sister did it for me. I just felt afraid of being [3]_____ because it's late.

Karen: That's not a good excuse, Danny. It's a matter of [4]_____. Let me tell you a story.

Danny: All right.

Karen: There was an old woodsman sitting beside a stream. His iron ax fell in the stream. Suddenly, a little fairy [5]_____. First, she gave the woodsman a golden ax. The woodsman said, "This is not mine." Next, she gave the woodsman a silver one. He still said that it was not his ax. Do you know what happened in the end?

Danny: No idea.

Karen: The little fairy was so [6]_____ by the woodsman's honesty that she decided to give him a new golden ax.

Danny: Sounds great! He got a new ax.

Karen: Hey, that's not the [7]_____. I just hope that you understand that being honest is very important.

Danny: Indeed. I learned my [8]_____ today. Thanks, Karen. Again, I'm sorry.

C *Practice the conversation with your partner.*

D *Recommend a book to your classmates that you've read. Tell them why you think it's worth reading. Make notes before sharing.*

Title: _____
Genre: _____
What's good: _____

117

Restrictive clauses limit the possible meaning of a preceding noun. Nonrestrictive clauses tell you something about a preceding noun, but they do not limit, or restrict, the meaning of that noun.

Restrictive

- Jim's sister **who/that is traveling in Europe** sent him a postcard.

  ➡️ *Jim has more than one sister. The one traveling in Europe sent him a postcard.*

Nonrestrictive

- Jim's sister, **who is traveling in Europe,** sent him a postcard.

  ➡️ *Jim has only one sister. She is traveling in Europe, and sent him a postcard.*

Restrictive

- Jason gave me the letter **which/that** was in a pink envelope.

  ➡️ *Jason gave me more than one letter. One of the letters was in a pink envelope.*

Nonrestrictive

- Jason gave me the letter, **which** was in a pink envelope.

  ➡️ *Jason gave me only one letter. The letter was in a pink envelope.*

👤 Live Grammar

Restrictive	Nonrestrictive
DO NOT have commas around clause	ALWAYS have commas around clause
Tell exactly which thing or person ➡️ The adjective clause CANNOT be omitted.	Give extra information ➡️ The adjective clause can be omitted.
Relative pronouns can be replaced with "that."	Relative pronouns CANNOT be replaced with "that."

Work It Out

A *Complete the sentences with **relative pronouns**.*

① The restaurant _____ my friend owns is in New York.

② I have a brother _____ is working in China.

    = I have more than one brother, and one of them is working in China.

③ They miss their only son, _____ is studying in the U.S. now.

B *Fill in the blanks with , or X.*

① I can't find the cheese _____ that you bought yesterday.

② I love my father _____ who always supports me.

③ Kevin _____ who likes to surf a lot _____ asked us to go to the beach with him.

④ My dog Bruce _____ which likes to play with me _____ is very cute.

⑤ I don't know the person _____ who you are talking about.

C *Combine the two sentences based on the hints given.*

① { My office is on the second floor.
    My office is very small. (which)

    _____ is very small.

② { Everyone is busy preparing for the New Year.
    New Year is just around the corner. (which)

    Everyone _____ .

③ { The cat is black.
    The cat loves to eat tuna. (which)

    _____ loves to eat tuna.

④ { Tina can speak three languages.
    Tina worked for a travel company. (who)

    _____ for a travel company.

The King and His Two Wives

🎧 2-29

A fable is a short story that tries to teach the reader a moral lesson. The most famous author of fables was a man called Aesop, who lived in Greece in the sixth century B.C. Let's examine one of his popular fables, "The King and His Two Wives."

Once upon a time, there was a king who had two wives. One was younger than
5 the king, and the other was older. Both wives loved the king, but the young wife was unhappy because the king's hair was starting to turn gray.

"I don't want a husband who looks so old," said the young wife. "People will think I'm his daughter!" So each night, she pulled out some of his gray hair.

"Ouch!" said the king. But he wanted his young wife to be happy, and he didn't
10 stop her. The older wife was happy that the king's hair was turning gray. "Now people will stop thinking I'm his mother," she said. And each morning, she pulled out some of the king's black hair.

"Ouch!" said the king. But he wanted his older wife to be happy, and he didn't stop her either.

15 Soon, the king had no hair left at all. Both of his wives cried when they saw how silly he looked. "Oh well," said the king. "If you try to <u>please</u> everyone, you end up pleasing no one."

Ⓐ *Fill in the blanks with the word choices given. Change the word form if necessary.*

> moral / examine / pull / author / century

1. She's the _____ of several successful children's books.

2. If you have a pet, you have a(n) _____ obligation to take care of it.

3. The museum reopened at the turn of the _____.

4. You shouldn't sign any contract before _____ its conditions carefully.

5. Mom! Jack is _____ my hair!

Ⓑ *Check the correct answers.*

1. Which of the following is NOT true about Aesop?
   - ☐ **a.** He is a famous author of fables.
   - ☐ **b.** He lived in Greece in the sixth century A.D.
   - ☐ **c.** He wrote the fable "The King and His Two Wives."

2. Why did the wives pull out the king's hair?
   - ☐ **a.** They wanted to make themselves look younger than their husband.
   - ☐ **b.** They wanted to make themselves look older than their husband.
   - ☐ **c.** They wanted to make themselves look as old as their husband.

3. Why didn't the king stop his wives?
   - ☐ **a.** He didn't mind having his hair pulled out.
   - ☐ **b.** He wanted to make them happy.
   - ☐ **c.** He thought they were being good to him.

4. What does the underlined word "please" mean?
   - ☐ **a.** Satisfy
   - ☐ **b.** Surprise
   - ☐ **c.** Upset

5. According to the fable, what happened to the king in the end?
   - ☐ **a.** His hair turned gray.
   - ☐ **b.** His hair turned black.
   - ☐ **c.** He lost all his hair.

After reading the fable, what lesson can you learn?

_____

_____

_____

WRITING

Read the following fable. Use your imagination to complete the story.

One day, a fox saw a crow sitting in a tree. The crow had a piece of cheese in her beak, which she was getting ready to eat. The fox wanted the cheese badly, so he thought about how he could get it. He walked to the foot of the tree and called up to the crow, saying ...

What lesson do you want your readers to learn after reading the fable?

CHALLENGE YOURSELF

Part I Pictures 🎧 2-30

Look at the picture and choose the best answer.

1.

☐ a ☐ b ☐ c

2.

☐ a ☐ b ☐ c

Part II Question & Response 🎧 2-31

Listen to the statement or question and choose the best response.

3. ☐ a ☐ b ☐ c   **5.** ☐ a ☐ b ☐ c
4. ☐ a ☐ b ☐ c   **6.** ☐ a ☐ b ☐ c

Part III Conversations 🎧 2-32

Listen to the conversation and answer the questions.

7. What are the students doing after lunch?
☐ a. Listening to a story
☐ b. Listening to music
☐ c. Writing a test

8. What does the man say about the woman's sister?
☐ a. He doesn't really like her that much.
☐ b. He thinks her behavior has changed.
☐ c. He's really worried about her.

9. What is the movie about?
☐ a. A man who works in the forest
☐ b. A man who is made of wood
☐ c. A man who writes ghost stories

10. What is Mandy's job?
☐ a. She's the manager at an advertising company.
☐ b. She's the manager at an entertainment company.
☐ c. She helps the manager.

Linguaporta Training

Let's review the unit with Linguaporta.

The Power of Words

WARM UP

TALK ABOUT THIS

Talk about these questions.

> What kind of compliments are best to give?

ACTIVATE

A *Listen and look at the pictures below. What do you think is happening in each picture?* 🔊 2-33

How do you feel when you receive a compliment?

B *Listen to the introduction again and number the sentences in order. Write the numbers in the box below.*

☐ You might compliment a classmate on their new shoes or a friend on their new perfume. But while physical compliments might boost your ego, the best compliments are those that focus on character.

☐ But did you know that giving these types of compliments can be even more powerful than receiving them?

1 You have likely received or given a compliment. Oftentimes, compliments are centered on appearance or style.

☐ Getting a compliment based on our inner qualities—who we are as people—is always more heartfelt and sincere. These compliments demonstrate that people understand us, care about us, and value our ideas.

☐ The act of giving a genuine compliment can boost your own positivity. The reason is simple: because you make someone else feel good! The positive energy you create will be met with even more positivity, like a smile or a "thank you." So don't delay—compliment someone today!

A Conversation between Friends

A *Watch the video clip and check the correct answers.* WEB動画 🖳

1. When did Ann go on a date with Ben?
   - ☐ **a.** Today
   - ☐ **b.** Yesterday
   - ☐ **c.** Last summer

2. Why does Ann like Ben?
   - ☐ **a.** Because he's easy to get along with.
   - ☐ **b.** Because he doesn't like to talk.
   - ☐ **c.** Because he's popular.

3. Who taught Ann how to cook?
   - ☐ **a.** Ben
   - ☐ **b.** Molly
   - ☐ **c.** Her mother

4. Why won't Ann continue to date Ben?
   - ☐ **a.** Because she doesn't like him.
   - ☐ **b.** Because he's moving away.
   - ☐ **c.** Because she is too busy with work.

B *Listen to the conversation and fill in the blanks.* 🎧 2-34 💻

Molly and Ann are having dinner at Ann's house.

Molly: Tell me all about your date with Ben [1]_____. What did you guys do?

Ann: We went to a coffee shop and talked. I like him. He's friendly and [2]_____.

Molly: Yeah, Ben's a super guy. He has a [3]_____ mind. He's pretty popular in class, too.

Ann: Really? Well, it's good that he's not like a lot of other guys who are popular.

Molly: I agree with you there. I'm glad that the two of you bonded. You know, this is the best meal I've had in [4]_____. Where did you learn to cook like this?

Ann: I'm glad you like it. Cooking is my hobby. I think I got it from my mom.

Molly: Well, this pasta is out of this [5]_____. I wish I had more time to devote to the kitchen, but it's hard for me to balance cooking with school.

Ann: You're a hard worker, and you've got lots of [6]_____. That's admirable.

Molly: So, let's get back to Ben. Will you go out with him again?

Ann: He's [7]_____ away after the summer. Didn't you know that?

Molly: I had no idea. That's too bad.

Ann: We're going to keep in [8]_____, though. We've got each other's e-mail addresses. He's going to e-mail me as soon as he arrives at his new place.

Molly: That's good. I'm happy to know that you've made a good friend.

C *Practice the conversation with your partner.*

D *Listen to the conversation. Who is Wendy?* 🎧 2-35

$$S. + be + adj. + \begin{cases} that + S. + V. \\ to\ V. \end{cases}$$

- I'm **happy** <u>that you're here</u>.
  ↳ *that clause*

- He was **angry** <u>that Jacob was late again</u>.
  ↳ *that clause*

- Mary was **sorry** <u>to hear the news</u>.
  ↳ *infinitive phrase*

$$S. + be + \begin{cases} adj. \\ N. \end{cases} + \begin{cases} (for\ sb/sth) + to\ V. \\ that + S. + V. \end{cases}$$

- It's **bad** <u>to skip breakfast every morning</u>.
  ↳ *infinitive phrase*

- It's **amazing** <u>that Mr. Jones ran a marathon at 80 years old</u>.
  ↳ *that clause*

- It's a **must** for people with diabetes <u>to be careful with their diet</u>.
  ↳ *infinitive phrase*

$$It + be + adj. + of\ sb + to\ V.$$

- It's <u>kind</u> **of** you <u>to offer to pay for the meal</u>.
  adj.   ↳ *infinitive phrase*

- It was <u>smart</u> **of** you <u>to sell your stock in that company</u>.
  adj.   ↳ *infinitive phrase*

- It was <u>clever</u> **of** him <u>to spot the mistake in the figures</u>.
  adj.   ↳ *infinitive phrase*

Work It Out

A *Fill in the blanks with **for** or **of**.*

① It's impossible _____ him to finish his work on time.

② It was brave _____ you to save the kid.

③ It was foolish _____ him to lie to the boss.

④ It's dangerous _____ people to talk on a cell phone while driving.

B *Rewrite the sentences.*

① Eating fruit every day is important.

= It _____

② Jules was careless to forget his wallet.

= It _____

③ To go home earlier is safe for me.

= It _____

④ To ask her out without her father's permission is impossible.

= It _____

GRAMMAR ❷ Subordinating Conjunctions: As Soon As

> As soon as + S. + V., S. + V.
> = S. + V. + as soon as + S. + V.

- <u>As soon as the bell rings</u>, <u>you can leave</u>.
  ↳*adverb clause*   ↳*main clause*

= You can leave **as soon as** the bell rings.

= You can leave **once/the moment** the bell rings.

- As soon as I get home, I'll start cooking dinner for everyone.
  ↳*use simple present when speaking about the future*

Work It Out

A *Combine the following sentences using **as soon as**.*

① I'll start reading the book. / It arrives.

_____

③ The door opened. / The cat ran out into the yard.

_____

② I went out for a run. / I got up.

_____

④ We clean off the table. / We can start to eat.

_____

What Riddles Can Teach Us

🎧 2-36

People often like to search for answers to things they don't understand, and riddles are one of the oldest ways to satisfy this desire. It's fun for us to solve riddles, but they're more than just games. They can also teach us <u>priceless</u> life lessons. Here are a few riddles for you to think about.

> **Q1** *What is always coming but never arrives?*
> Tomorrow.

5   Everyone has dreams, but many people get caught up in their day-to-day lives and put off important things until tomorrow, which never comes. People who do this may never achieve their goals. Therefore, it's best to prepare for the future by doing a little bit every day.

> **Q2** *Everyone wants more of it to feel special, but the more you have of it, the less special you feel. What is it?*
> Knowledge.

We start learning as soon as we're born, and the process of learning continues for the
10 rest of our lives. When people are young, they tend to think they know it all!

As we age, we start to realize how much more there is to know. In this regard, knowledge is humbling.

Spend a few minutes thinking about these and other riddles. The lessons they teach are useful, and they might help you out later in life.

130

Ⓐ *Fill in the blanks with the word choices given. Change the word form if necessary.*

> achieve / regard / knowledge / desire / riddle

1. After so many years of war, there was a great _____ for peace.
2. I have nothing further to say in this _____.
3. See if you can solve this _____.
4. Ted has worked hard to _____ his goal.
5. Natalie has a limited _____ of Chinese.

Ⓑ *Check the correct answers.*

1. What does the underlined word "priceless" mean?
   - ☐ a. Precious
   - ☐ b. Replaceable
   - ☐ c. Cheap

2. According to the article, what can riddles teach us?
   - ☐ a. How to search for things
   - ☐ b. Lessons about life
   - ☐ c. Old ways to solve problems

3. Why do people put things off?
   - ☐ a. They choose to abandon their dreams.
   - ☐ b. They spend too much time thinking about the past.
   - ☐ c. They get too involved in other things.

4. How is it best to prepare for the future?
   - ☐ a. Focus more on your past
   - ☐ b. Wait until you have more time to prepare
   - ☐ c. Accomplish small things every day

5. When do people first begin learning?
   - ☐ a. When they're young
   - ☐ b. When they're born
   - ☐ c. When they get older

Here are some funny riddles for you to solve. Write the answers in the blanks.

① What can fly without wings?
_____

② What do you call a bear without an ear?
_____

③ If you are running in a race and pass the second-place runner, what place are you in?
_____

131

WRITING

Read the following instructions and write your own riddles.

 Step 1

Choose an answer first!

Make sure your answer is something simple, like an object or an animal. For example, a good answer would be "tea," or perhaps "bees."

 Step 2

Brainstorm about your answer.

Write down everything you can think of about your answer.

Tea	Bees
Drink, plant, hot, cup, caffeine ...	Insect, honey, buzz, sting, hive ...

 Step 3

Think like your object.

Try describing the world from your answer's point of view. What do you see? What do you hear? Where do you live? What do you do? What do you feel?

Tea	Bees
I live in a cup. I feel hot. I hear people drinking. I like to ...	I see flowers. I hear buzzing noises. I like to make honey. I feel ...

 Step 4

Write your riddle!

"I start life as a plant, and I end life in a cup." *(Answer: tea)*

"I like to buzz, buzz, buzz!" *(Answer: bees)*

 Step 1

 Step 2

 Step 3

 Step 4

CHALLENGE YOURSELF

Look at the picture and choose the best answer.

1.

☐ a ☐ b ☐ c

2.

☐ a ☐ b ☐ c

Part II Question & Response 🔊 2-38

Listen to the statement or question and choose the best response.

3. ☐ a ☐ b ☐ c   5. ☐ a ☐ b ☐ c

4. ☐ a ☐ b ☐ c   6. ☐ a ☐ b ☐ c

Part III Conversations 🔊 2-39

Listen to the conversation and answer the questions.

7. What will the man order?
   ☐ a. Some noodles
   ☐ b. Meat
   ☐ c. A salad

8. What do we know about the man?
   ☐ a. He doesn't want to go out.
   ☐ b. He hates staying at home.
   ☐ c. He's going out with the woman.

9. What is said about Annie Winston?
   ☐ a. The man dislikes her.
   ☐ b. Many people like her.
   ☐ c. Her songs are not popular.

10. What do we know about Matt?
    ☐ a. He's not good at cooking.
    ☐ b. He has gone to culinary school.
    ☐ c. The meal he cooked is delicious.

UNIT
12

THE POWER OF WORDS

Linguaporta Training

Let's review the unit with Linguaporta.

Part I 🎧 2-40

Listen to the statement or question and check the best response.

1. ☐ a ☐ b ☐ c   3. ☐ a ☐ b ☐ c
2. ☐ a ☐ b ☐ c   4. ☐ a ☐ b ☐ c

Part II 🎧 2-41

Listen to the conversation and check the correct answer.

1. What does the man say about Emmy?
   - ☐ **a.** She's famous.
   - ☐ **b.** She's thoughtful.
   - ☐ **c.** She's sad.

2. Which of the following statements is correct?
   - ☐ **a.** The woman is going to get married next month.
   - ☐ **b.** The man and the woman are a couple.
   - ☐ **c.** James will marry his girlfriend soon.

3. What can we say about the man?
   - ☐ **a.** He got a good grade on the exam.
   - ☐ **b.** He likes bright colors.
   - ☐ **c.** He's very positive.

4. How does Mike's mom feel?
   - ☐ **a.** Proud
   - ☐ **b.** Happy
   - ☐ **c.** Bothered

Part III 🎧 2-42

Listen to the short passage and check the correct picture.

1.

 ☐ a

☐ b

 ☐ c

2.

 ☐ a

 ☐ b

 ☐ c

Part IV

Fill in the blanks.

> pleasant / punish / happened to / put off / devotes / upset / lessons / search / married / wish

1. Frank had a very _____ vacation.

2. Could you help me _____ for my phone?

3. Anne was _____ that her friend had lied to her.

4. I _____ be in town, so I decided to come over and visit you.

5. Are you _____ or single?

6. Val made a _____ on a falling star.

7. My parents will probably _____ me for failing this test.

8. That was a hard experience, but I learned some _____ from it.

9. Matt _____ doing his homework until late in the evening.

10. Ryan works during the day and _____ his evenings to studying.

Part V

Check the correct answer.

1. Individuals _____ are popular usually have a good people skills.
   - ☐ **a.** which
   - ☐ **b.** whom
   - ☐ **c.** whose
   - ☐ **d.** who

2. Jack likes to stay in shape, so he goes swimming _____ he can.
   - ☐ **a.** as soon as
   - ☐ **b.** as often as
   - ☐ **c.** as late as
   - ☐ **d.** as usual as

3. It was difficult for Chris _____ a perfect gift for his girlfriend. Therefore, he decided to ask his sister for advice.
   - ☐ **a.** found
   - ☐ **b.** finds
   - ☐ **c.** to find
   - ☐ **d.** by finding

4. Many experts advise against _____ the midnight oil _____.
   - ☐ **a.** to burn / studying
   - ☐ **b.** burning / studying
   - ☐ **c.** burning / study
   - ☐ **d.** burned / studied

5. Earl _____ is a fantastic cook, has a huge kitchen in his house.
   - ☐ **a.** who
   - ☐ **b.** , who
   - ☐ **c.** whose
   - ☐ **d.** , whose

6. Andy wanted to call Rose. _____, he didn't have her phone number.
   - ☐ **a.** Because
   - ☐ **b.** However
   - ☐ **c.** And
   - ☐ **d.** So

7. The rent is quite reasonable. _____, the location is perfect.
   - ☐ **a.** Thus
   - ☐ **b.** However
   - ☐ **c.** Instead
   - ☐ **d.** In addition

8. Oliver bought a Christmas gift _____ his girlfriend.
   - ☐ **a.** for
   - ☐ **b.** to
   - ☐ **c.** of
   - ☐ **d.** on

9. The music _____ beautiful. I like it very much.
   - ☐ **a.** looks
   - ☐ **b.** tastes
   - ☐ **c.** sounds
   - ☐ **d.** smells

10. It was careless _____ Bob to forget to bring his wallet.
    - ☐ **a.** to
    - ☐ **b.** of
    - ☐ **c.** for
    - ☐ **d.** on

Read the article and check the correct answer.

There are many expressions in English that can be traced back to Greek mythology. By looking into the stories behind these idioms, we can better understand their meaning. According to legend, the Greeks and their enemies, the Trojans,
5 fought each other in the Trojan War. Among the greatest warriors fighting for Greece was a man named Achilles, who was so powerful that he seemed to be invincible. However, he was eventually killed by an arrow shot through his heel. This led to the phrase "Achilles' heel," meaning someone or something's
10 weak spot.

Just before the end of the war, the Greeks built an enormous wooden horse and left it outside the city of Troy. The Trojans believed the gift was a peace offering and took it through the gates of the city. However, there were Greek soldiers hiding
15 inside, who came out at night and attacked, leading to a Greek victory in the war. This is the origin of the idiom "beware of Greeks bearing gifts."

Likewise, this is where the term "Trojan horse" comes from, referring to something used to bring about defeat through
20 deception. Nowadays, this term is also used to describe a program that seems harmless but actually compromises data on someone's computer.

Achilles' heel

Trojan horse

1. According to the article, who is Achilles?
   - ☐ **a.** A king of Greece
   - ☐ **b.** A warrior fighting against Greece
   - ☐ **c.** A warrior fighting against the Trojans

2. What does the underlined phrase "Achilles' heel" mean?
   - ☐ **a.** An invincible warrior
   - ☐ **b.** A small problem that can result in failure
   - ☐ **c.** A weak person

3. What does the underlined idiom "beware of Greeks bearing gifts" mean?
   - ☐ **a.** You should forgive enemies who bring you presents.
   - ☐ **b.** You should make peace with people who bring you presents.
   - ☐ **c.** You should be suspicious of people who are suddenly kind to you.

4. Which sentence is true?

  ☐ **a.** The term "Trojan horse" comes from Greek mythology.

  ☐ **b.** Trojan soldiers were hiding inside the huge wooden horse.

  ☐ **c.** The term "Trojan horse" was invented only recently.

5. What is the best title for this article?

  ☐ **a.** The History of the Trojan War

  ☐ **b.** The Origin of "Trojan Horse"

  ☐ **c.** Idioms from Greek Mythology

Part VII

Combine the sentences with the hints given.

1. The woman is a teacher. She lives next door. *(who)*

_____

2. How's the project going? It's due on Friday. *(which)*

_____

3. The police caught the robber. He tried to run away. *(who)*

_____

4. My mother thinks I study too hard. You met her last Tuesday. *(whom)*

_____

Look at the following three pictures. Write about what happened to Martha in 40-60 words.

_____

_____

_____

_____

_____

リンガポルタのご案内

LINGUAPORTA

> リンガポルタ連動テキストをご購入の学生さんは、「リンガポルタ」を無料でご利用いただけます！

本テキストで学習していただく内容に準拠した問題を、オンライン学習システム「リンガポルタ」で学習していただくことができます。PCだけでなく、スマートフォンやタブレットでも学習できます。単語や文法、リスニング力などをよりしっかり身に付けていただくため、ぜひ積極的に活用してください。

リンガポルタの利用にはアカウントとアクセスコードの登録が必要です。登録方法については下記ページにアクセスしてください。

https://www.seibido.co.jp/linguaporta/register.html

本テキスト「Live Escalate Book 2: Trekking」のアクセスコードは下記です。

7222-2045-1231-0365-0003-006a-Q97F-RUKB

・リンガポルタの学習機能（画像はサンプルです。また、すべてのテキストに以下の4つの機能が用意されているわけではありません）

多肢選択

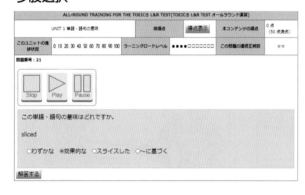

空所補充（音声を使っての聞き取り問題も可能）

単語並びかえ（マウスや手で単語を移動）

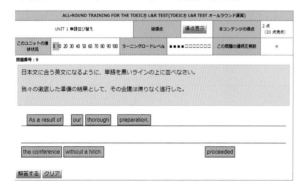

マッチング（マウスや手で単語を移動）

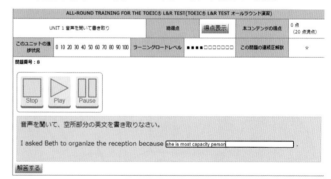

Web動画のご案内　**StreamLine**

本テキストの映像は、オンラインでのストリーミング再生になります。下記URLよりご利用ください。なお**有効期限は、はじめてログインした時点から1年半**です。

http://st.seibido.co.jp

① ログイン画面

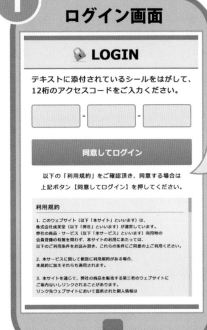

巻末に添付されているシールをはがして、アクセスコードをご入力ください。

② メニュー画面

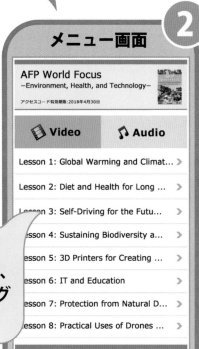

「Video」または「Audio」を選択すると、それぞれストリーミング再生ができます。

③ 再生画面

推奨動作環境

【PC OS】
Windows 7~ ／ Mac 10.8~

【Mobile OS】
iOS ／ Android ※Androidの場合は4.x~が推奨

【Desktop ブラウザ】
Internet Explorer 9~ / Firefox / Chrome / Safari / Microsoft Edge

TEXT PRODUCTION STAFF

edited by	編集
Takashi Kudo	工藤 隆志

cover design by	表紙デザイン
Nobuyoshi Fujino	藤野 伸芳

text design by	本文デザイン
Ruben Frosali	ルーベン・フロサリ

CD PRODUCTION STAFF

recorded by	吹き込み者
Rachel Walzer (AmE)	レイチェル・ワルザー（アメリカ英語）
Howard Colefield (AmE)	ハワード・コールフィルド（アメリカ英語）
Dominic Allen (AmE)	ドミニク・アレン（アメリカ英語）
Karen Haedrich (AmE)	カレン・ヘドリック（アメリカ英語）

Live Escalate Book 2: Trekking

2021年1月10日　初版発行
2024年2月10日　第7刷発行

著　　者　角山 照彦
　　　　　Live ABC editors

発 行 者　佐野 英一郎

発 行 所　株式会社 成美堂
　　　　　〒101-0052　東京都千代田区神田小川町3-22
　　　　　TEL 03-3291-2261　FAX 03-3293-5490
　　　　　https://www.seibido.co.jp

印刷・製本　(株)加藤文明社

ISBN 978-4-7919-7222-7　　　　　　　　　　Printed in Japan